To Claire

With love from

Mummy and Daddy

3 July 1977

THE GREATEST
Bible Stories

THE GREATEST
Bible Stories

Edited by Howard Jennings

OCTOPUS

The Old Testament

CONTENTS

This edition first published 1977 by Octopus Books Limited,
59 Grosvenor Street, London, W1.

Text © 1973 Octopus Books Limited
Illustrations © 1973 L'Esperto S.p.A.,
Milan-Octopus Books Limited, London

ISBN 0 7064 0633 8

Produced and Printed by Mandarin Publishers Limited.
22A Westlands Road, Quarry Bay, Hong Kong

The Creation

BEFORE you or I were made, or the continents and seas, or the earth or the stars or the universe or space itself, God thought he would create the world. First he made the heavens and the earth, a mass of whirling clouds and vapours, without form or solidity. And everything was dark.

God saw that he had hardly begun. He said, "Let there be light," and there was light and God divided the light from the darkness and made day and night.

But there was no shape to anything that he had made so God divided the sky from the earth, and put one on top of the other.

On earth God gathered all the waters together to make the seas. He made the dry land and made grass grow on the land. He made plants that give seeds, and trees that give fruit. And when he saw what he had made, he liked it.

To mark the seasons, the days and the years, God made the sun and the moon and stars to shine in the sky, and God was pleased with these.

Then God made creatures to live on the earth. He made great whales, and the smaller fish, and every creature that moves in the sea, and he made the birds. He was glad that he had made them, and he blessed them and said, "Have children, and fill the sea and the air."

He also made all the other countless creatures that live on the earth—wild beasts and insects and things that crawl in the soil. And he liked what he had made.

Finally God said, "I will make man. I will make him in my own shape and I will give him power over all the creatures I have made." So God made man and woman. He blessed them and told them to have children, to live on the earth and to rule over it.

God said, "I have given you plants to eat. And I have given plants for the cattle and for the other beasts, and for every living creature that moves on the earth."

Then God looked at everything that he had made; and it pleased him.

In six days God had made the heavens and the earth and all its plants and creatures. His work was finished.

So on the seventh day, God rested. He blessed the seventh day, and made it a holy day for ever.

The Garden of Eden and the Serpent

WHEN the first rains had watered the earth, God made man. He took clay and moulded it into his own shape. Then he breathed life into the clay, and gave man a living soul. This first man was called Adam. God gave him a beautiful garden to live in, called the Garden of Eden, in which God had planted flowers and fruit trees of every kind. God told Adam that he could eat the fruit of every tree in the garden except one, the tree of the knowledge of good and evil. "Eat from that tree," God said to Adam, "and you will surely die."

Adam was content with his life in the garden, but God saw that of all the creatures he had made, only man had no partner. So God put Adam into a deep sleep, and while he was sleeping, God took a rib from Adam's side. From this rib God made a woman, whose name was Eve, to be a wife and a companion to Adam.

Adam and Eve lived happily in the garden. But there was one creature in the garden who wished to make trouble between God and man. This was the serpent, who was the most cunning of all the creatures God had made. One day the serpent found Eve alone in the garden, and he whispered in her ear, "You will not die if you eat the fruit of the tree of knowledge of good and evil. You will understand everything, and you will both be like gods."

Eve believed the serpent, and wanted to be a god. She took the fruit and ate it, and gave it to Adam, and he ate it too. At once everything changed. They felt guilty and unhappy for the first time. Also, they were ashamed of their nakedness, so they sewed fig leaves together to cover themselves up.

That evening, Adam and Eve heard God walking in the garden, and they hid them-

selves among the trees. "Where are you?" God called out to Adam. Then Adam had to come out of hiding. "I heard your voice," he said to God, "and I was afraid because I was naked, so I hid myself."

"Who told you that you were naked?" God asked him. "Have you eaten the fruit of the forbidden tree?" "The woman made me do it," Adam said.

"Why did you do it?" God asked Eve. "The serpent made me do it," she replied.

God grew very angry and put a curse on the serpent. Then he turned to Adam and Eve. "Because you have disobeyed me," he said, "I will send you out of the Garden of Eden into the wilderness, where life will be hard for you. Woman will give birth in pain, and man will have to work hard to raise crops, until he dies. I made you out of dust, and you will return to dust."

So Adam and Eve had to leave the garden where they had been so happy, and God set an angel to guard it with a flaming sword so that they could never return.

9

Cain and Abel

LIFE was hard for Adam and Eve outside the garden, as God had said it would be. Eve gave birth to a son, whom she called Cain. Soon afterwards, she had another baby whom she named Abel. Now she and Adam had two sons to help them grow their crops and take care of their animals. When the boys grew up Cain became a farmer and worked in the fields, raising crops, while Abel became a shepherd and looked after the sheep.

Adam and Eve used to show their love and respect for God by offering sacrifices to him. They would build an altar out of stones, light a fire, and then kill the finest young lamb or goat in their flock by cutting its throat and pouring the blood into a bowl. Then they would burn its body in the fire. They brought other offerings too—fruit, vegetables and grain, but always the gift they sacrificed was the best of its kind, to say Thank you to God, who had provided it.

One day, Cain and Abel made sacrifices too. Cain brought grain from his harvest and Abel brought young lambs from his flock. God was pleased with Abel's sacrifice because he had offered it gladly; but he knew that Cain had not really wanted to make his offering, so he did not accept it. This made Cain very angry. "Why are you cross?" God said to Cain. "If you do well and give gladly, your offering will be accepted, but if your thoughts are full of evil, then evil will rule you."

Then Cain was not only angry but jealous of Abel, and when they were next out in the fields together he beat him so badly that he killed him.

When Cain came home, God said to him, "Where is your brother Abel?" and Cain replied, "I don't know—it's not my job to know where he is."

"What have you done?" God said to Cain. "I know you have killed your brother—his blood is crying out to me from the earth. From now on you will never again be able to farm, or bring in the harvest. You must wander like a stranger for the rest of your days, and never belong anywhere."

"That means I will never see you again and never have a home again, and everyone who finds me will want to kill me," Cain pleaded with God. "I don't think I can bear such a dreadful punishment."

God marked Cain with a special mark so that men would know he had killed his brother and no one would kill him, and this meant he had to undergo the punishment of living without friends for the rest of his life.

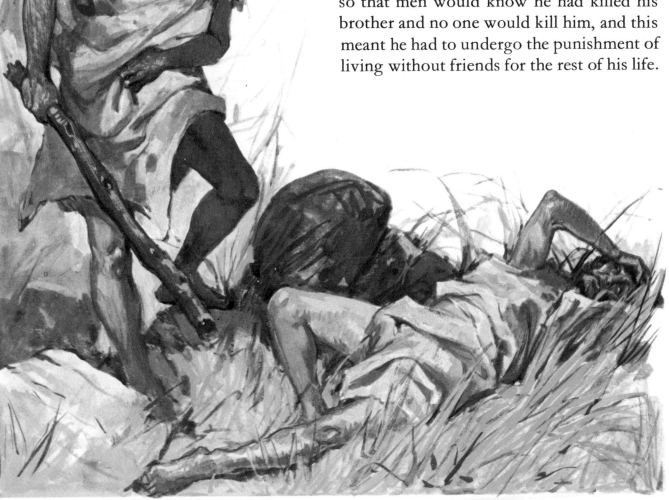

Noah's Ark

Years passed, and many people lived on the earth, but they had become very wicked. They argued and fought and stole and lied, and cheated one another so badly that God became sorry that he had made people who were causing such trouble and he decided he would destroy them all.

But there was among them one man who was good. His name was Noah, and God loved him. So he spoke to Noah and told him what he was going to do. He would send so much rain that there would be a great flood, and it would drown everything on the earth.

When Noah heard this he was very frightened, but God said, "Don't worry, Noah, you are a good man, and I won't destroy you or your wife, or your sons, or

their wives. But you must do exactly as I tell you, so that when the flood comes you will be saved."

God told Noah to build a great boat called an ark. It was to be 450 feet long, 75 feet wide and 45 feet high. It was to be made of cypress wood, covered with reeds and coated with tar both inside and out. Noah cut and sawed, and bent and shaped. He built three decks, cut a large door in one side and put a window in the top.

The people who lived nearby laughed at Noah while he was building the ark. "Why build a boat here – we're nowhere near the sea. You must be mad," they said.

But Noah paid no attention.

"This big ark is not only for you," God said to Noah. "I want you to go out and collect a male and a female of every kind of animal and bird and reptile, and take them into the ark with you. Now go and gather all the food you can find for you and for them. You will need enough for a long voyage."

When Noah's neighbours saw Noah and his family piling stores of fruit and grain, leaves and hay, inside the ark, they jeered louder than ever. But Noah and his family paid no attention and went on with their work. Two of every kind of animal and bird and reptile eat a lot of food, and very soon it would begin to rain.

When all the stores were ready, Noah and his wife and his sons and his sons' wives went out to collect the animals. They followed Noah into the ark, two by two. As soon as every one of them was safely on board, the first drops of rain started to fall.

It rained and it rained. Quite soon the ark began to float, but the water rose and rose, until it covered even the mountaintops and every living creature that was not on the ark was drowned. But it still rained. It rained for 40 days and 40 nights, and after it had finally stopped raining, the flood waters went on covering the whole earth for 150 days.

Then God thought of Noah and the ark, and he made a strong wind blow, and the flood waters gradually went down. At last the ark came to rest on the top of a mountain. Noah began to send out birds, to see if they could find dry land, but they could find no place to perch. Finally one day Noah sent out a dove, and that evening the dove came back with an olive twig in its beak. Some parts of the land were dry again. The next time Noah released the dove, it did not come back at all, which showed Noah that it was now safe to leave the ark.

So Noah and his family, and all the creatures they had taken with them, came out of the ark onto dry land, and Noah built an altar and offered a sacrifice of thanksgiving. God was pleased, and he blessed Noah and his family and told them to have many children and fill the earth with people again.

"I will make a promise to you and all your children," God said. "I will never again send a flood to destroy everything. I will put a rainbow in every rain cloud, and whenever you see it you can remember my promise, which will last for ever."

The Tower of Babel

HERE was once a time when everyone spoke the same language and understood one another perfectly. In those days the people of the earth wandered westwards, looking for a place to settle.

When they came to a plain in the land of Shinar, they said, "How beautiful a city would look here in place of this wilderness! Instead of trees and grass we will have houses and avenues. We will build a great wall around the city, to protect us. We will make domes that gleam in the sun, and gardens and fountains to cool us after our work. We will sink wells deep into the earth and build towers that reach into the sky. We will begin by building a tower that will be so high that it will reach to God himself."

After a while God came to look at their city and their tower, and was very angry. "If men can do this," he said to himself, "there is nothing they won't be able to do. I will confuse their speech, and make them all speak different languages, so that they won't be able to understand one another."

Suddenly, not one person could understand what anybody else was saying. There was terrible confusion in the city. All the work stopped, and the people went off in different directions and scattered themselves over the face of the earth.

The city, which was left unfinished, was given the name of Babel, because it was the place where God had made a babble out of the inhabitants' speech.

The Promise to Abram

HERE was once a man called Abram, who lived in the city of Haran, in Mesopotamia. Abram was a good man, and he loved his wife Sarai, but they had never had any children. One day God said to Abram, "You must leave your house, and your relations, and your country – I am going to show you a new country. I have chosen you to be the father of a great new nation, and I will bless you and make your name so famous that men will always remember it. I will bless everyone who blesses you, and curse anyone who curses you. All the families on earth will pray to be blessed as you are blessed."

Abram did as God had commanded him, and set out from Haran, taking his wife Sarai, his nephew Lot, and his flocks, his money and his servants. They journeyed until they reached the land of Canaan, where the Canaanites were living. There God appeared to Abram again, and said, "I give this land to you and to your family for ever." Abram built an altar at the spot where he had heard God's voice, and offered a sacrifice. Then he travelled on, towards the Negeb desert.

There was a great famine in the land of Canaan, so Abram took his family to Egypt, to live for a while in the land that was ruled by the Pharaohs. On the way there Abram said to Sarai, "You are so beautiful that I am afraid the Egyptians will kill me so that they can make you one of Pharaoh's wives. Let's say that you are my sister, not my wife, and then they will treat me well so as to gain favour with you." So they agreed on this plan.

When they arrived in Egypt, just as Abram had expected, Pharaoh's courtiers admired Sarai's beauty and told their king that he should take her as his wife. Then Pharaoh sent Abram many gifts, sheep and cattle and donkeys and camels, and slaves, both male and female, and he took Sarai into his household with the intention of making her one of his wives.

But God at once made Pharaoh and all his household fall ill with a great sickness. Pharaoh realized that Abram's God was doing this to him on account of Sarai, and he called Abram to him and said: "Why did you let me make this dreadful mistake? You should have told me she was your wife. Now take her and go away."

So Abram left Egypt and went back to the Negeb with Sarai and his nephew Lot, and all the silver and gold and cattle in their possession. He was now a wealthy man, for Pharaoh had been generous with his gifts, and had not insisted that Abram give them

back before he left Egypt.

God said to Abram, "Look up, and look far into the distance, north and south and east and west. I will give the land as far as you can see to you and to your descendants for ever. I will make them as countless as the grains of dust on the ground. Now go and explore the land, for it is rightfully yours."

Then Abram travelled the length and breadth of the land God had given him, and built an altar to God in the plains of Hebron.

The Pillar of Salt

On their return from Egypt, Abram and Lot parted company. Abram went to Canaan, and Lot chose the plain of Jordan, settling near Sodom.

Now the people of the cities of Sodom and Gomorrah were known for the degenerate lives they led. God wanted to destroy the cities, but first he sent two messengers to Sodom to see whether any good men still lived there, for he would have spared them all if there had been even ten men worth saving.

The messengers found Lot sitting near the city gate. He invited them to eat with him and to sleep at his house.

While they were eating, the men of Sodom came and beat on Lot's door.

"Bring out those strangers," they cried. "We want to have our fun with them."

"No," Lot shouted back, "these men are my guests."

"Then we'll kill you instead," cried the men, and they tried to break down the door to get at Lot. But God struck every one of them blind where they stood so they could not find the door.

"Flee for your life," God's messengers said to Lot, "and take your wife and your daughters with you. These people must be punished, but don't look back and don't stop, or you will be swept away like them."

Then God made a storm like an erupting volcano, and fire and ashes rained down onto Sodom and Gomorrah, and earthquakes shook the cities to the ground. Everything was destroyed, except Lot fleeing with his wife and daughters.

But Lot's wife stopped and looked back, reluctant to leave the pleasures of the city—and she was turned into a pillar of salt.

Abram and Isaac

WHEN Abram was an old man God appeared to him in a vision and said, "Don't be afraid, Abram, for I am going to give you great rewards. Look at the stars in the sky. You will have as many descendants as there are stars."

"But, Lord," said Abram, "Sarai and I have never had a child, and now we are too old to have one."

"Trust me," God said to him, "and I will make you a promise. For a time your family will live in a foreign land and men will be cruel to them. But I will punish the nation that makes them into slaves, and send them home again as wealthy men. I give this land of Canaan, from the Nile to the Euphrates river, to you and to your descendants for all time. Your name will no longer be Abram but Abraham, for you will be the father of many nations. Your part of the promise is that you will have every male child born in your household circumcised. I will not accept an uncircumcized man as a member of your family."

Then God said, "As for Sarai, your wife, she too will have a new name, Sarah. Old as she is, I will bless her so that she will give you a son, and you must call him Isaac. Ishmael, the son you have had by your slave woman Hagar, will be the father of princes and of a great nation. But it is Isaac, the

son you and Sarah will have, whose children will fulfil the promise I have made."

Abraham and Sarah waited quietly for God's promise to be fulfilled. One day three men appeared at their tent, and Abraham gave them food to eat and water to refresh themselves. "Your son will be born in the spring," said the men, who were messengers from God.

Spring came, and Sarah gave birth to a son. They called him Isaac, and Abraham circumcized him.

When Isaac had grown into a boy God decided to test Abraham's faith. He ordered him to take his son into the mountains and kill him, instead of the lamb he usually killed, as a sacrifice to God.

Abraham loved Isaac dearly, but he also loved God. He set off for the mountains with a very heavy heart, and Isaac came

with him, carrying the wood for the fire. When they came to the hills Isaac said to his father, "Father, we've come all this way, but we didn't bring a young lamb to kill in God's honour." "God will provide the sacrifice," said Abraham.

When they came to the right place, Abraham built an altar out of stones and lit a fire on it. Then he tied Isaac up, and was just about to raise his knife to kill the terrified boy when God called to him to stop.

"There is a ram nearby which has caught its horns in a bush. Offer that as a sacrifice instead of your beloved son. Now I know beyond any doubt the extent of your faith and love for me."

Abraham untied Isaac and held him close to him. They caught the ram and sacrificed it as God had told them to. Then the father and son went home together, rejoicing.

Jacob and Esau

I SAAC married Rebecca from Haran, his home city, but they were sad because they had not had children. Then Isaac prayed to God for a child, and God listened to Isaac and answered his prayers. Rebecca gave birth to twin boys. Before they were born God said to Rebecca, "Your sons will be the fathers of two nations. One will be stronger than the other and the older will be the servant of the younger."

The boys were born and their parents called them Esau and Jacob. Esau, the elder, became a hunter and roamed the plains in search of deer. Jacob preferred to stay at home among his father's tents. Isaac's favourite was Esau, but Rebecca favoured Jacob.

One day Esau returned from hunting ravenously hungry and impatient to eat. "Let me have some of that bread and soup you have made," he said to Jacob. "Not until you have sold me your right as first-born son to inherit most of what our father owns," Jacob replied.

Esau barely took time to think over Jacob's demand. His birthright seemed nothing in comparison with his need for a hearty meal at once. "I'm nearly dead with hunger and exhaustion—what use is my birthright to me now?" he thought. So he swore an oath and gave his birthright to Jacob in exchange for the food his brother had cooked.

Time went by and Isaac became nearly blind. One day he called Esau to him and said: "I am old and my life will soon be over. Take your bow and arrows and shoot me a deer on the plains. Cook the meat the way I like it, and then bring it to me to eat, and I will give you a special blessing."

Rebecca had overheard Isaac's words and as soon as Esau had set off for the hunt she said to Jacob, "Now listen to me, and do exactly as I say. Pick out two young kids from our herd of goats. I will cook them the way your father likes, in a sauce made with bitter herbs, and then you can take them to him and say you are Esau. Then he will give you the special blessing that a father gives the son who will be his heir."

"But Esau is hairy," Jacob said, "and my skin is smooth. I know my father can't see well, but as soon as he touches me he will know that I am trying to trick him, and he will curse me instead of blessing me." "Don't worry," said his mother, "just bring me the kids."

So Jacob killed two kids and Rebecca skinned them and cooked them with herbs. She covered Jacob's arms and neck with the skins and dressed him in some of Esau's clothes. Then she put the dish of meat into his hands, and he took it to his father and asked for his blessing.

"Come close and let me feel you, my son," said Isaac, "so that I can be sure you really are Esau." Jacob came and kneeled by his father so that Isaac could touch him with his hands. "You sound like Jacob," his father said, "but your arms feel like Esau's," and he stroked the hairy skins. "Are you

really Esau?" he asked, and Jacob lied and said he was.

Isaac ate the meat Jacob had brought and then he asked his son to kiss him. As he put his arms around Jacob, he recognized the smell of Esau on his clothes and felt certain he was embracing his first-born son, so he gave him the special blessing:

"May God always give you water and the rich harvest of the earth. People will serve you and nations will honour you. You will be the leader among your brothers, and they must do as you say. I set my curse on anyone who does harm to you and give my blessing to everyone who helps you."

Jacob had no sooner left his father than Esau came back from the hunt, carrying a deer he had killed. He cooked the meat the way his father liked it, and then he brought it to him and asked for his blessing.

"But who are you?" asked Isaac, and

Esau replied, "I am Esau, your first-born son."

Isaac began to tremble. "Who was it," he asked, "who brought me the meat just now? I ate it and blessed *him*, and that blessing must stand."

Then Esau cried out loudly and bitterly, "Bless me too, father."

"Your brother has taken the blessing," Isaac answered. "I have made him your chief and given him everything I have."

"Haven't you any blessing left for me?" cried Esau. "Please bless me too, father."

"You will always live without having much," Isaac said to him. "You will earn your living by fighting, and you will have to serve your brother. But in time you will break away and be a free man."

From then on Esau hated Jacob and planned to kill him. Esau said to himself, "My father Isaac will soon die, and then I will kill my brother, for he has cheated me and taken both my birthright and my father's special blessing."

Jacob's Ladder

REBECCA soon found out that Esau was planning to kill his brother Jacob, and she at once became very frightened. She knew Esau might make an attack on his brother at any time, and that if Jacob fought back she might then lose both of her sons.

"You must leave here at once," she told Jacob, "and you ought to go as far away as you can. My brother Laban still lives in Haran. Go to him; he will give you a home for a while. Then, when Esau's anger has died down, I will send you a message saying you can come home again."

So Jacob decided he ought to leave Beersheba as soon as he could. But his mother told his father what he intended to do, and the evening before Jacob left, Isaac sent for him and said:

"I want you to choose a wife while you are in Haran, from among our own people. I don't want you to marry a woman from the land of Canaan. God will bless you, you will have a whole nation of descendants, and this land of Canaan will be yours, just as God promised your grandfather Abraham."

So Jacob set out by himself for Haran. Although his father's blessing had made him the heir to all Isaac's flocks and herds, he carried nothing with him, except some food for the journey. His only clothes were the ones he was wearing. He walked all day and late into the evening until he was too tired to go on. So he stopped to rest. He made a pillow out of a stone that was lying nearby. Then he wrapped himself in his cloak and lay down to sleep.

He dreamed that he saw a ladder which reached from the ground right up to heaven, and that angels were moving up and down it. God seemed to be standing beside him, and he said to Jacob:

"I give the land where you are lying to you and to your descendants. They will be as countless as the dust on the earth, and will spread far and wide, north and south and east and west. I will be with you and protect you, wherever you go, and I will bring you back again to this land, to fulfil the promise I made to Abraham, your grandfather."

Then Jacob woke up, and at once he knew that he had truly been in the presence of God. He took the stone he had used as a pillow and set it up as a sacred pillar, and poured oil over it as a thanksgiving to God.

Jacob and Rachel

As JACOB travelled towards Haran, he wondered what life would be like among all the relations he did not know, and whom he would find to marry. He had almost reached the city when he saw a well with several flocks of sheep gathered around it. He asked the shepherds who were minding the sheep where they came from, and they told him they were from Haran. "Do you know my uncle Laban?" Jacob asked them. "Indeed we do," they replied, "and here comes his daughter Rachel with his flock."

When Rachel came up to the well, Jacob helped her to water her sheep. Then he told her who he was, and she at once ran home to tell her father. Laban hurried out to greet his nephew and welcomed him to his home.

So Jacob stayed with Laban and worked for him. "You shouldn't work for nothing just because you are my nephew," Laban said to him one day. "How can I repay you?" "I will work seven years for nothing," Jacob replied, "if you will give me your daughter Rachel as my wife."

Now Laban had two daughters: Leah, the elder, was plain and slow and Rachel, the younger, was graceful and beautiful. Laban said to Jacob, "You will make a good husband. Work for me for seven years and then you can take Rachel as your wife." So Jacob worked for Laban, and the years seemed like days because he loved Rachel so much.

When his time was up, Jacob said to Laban, "I have served you well. Now give me Rachel so that we can be married and live together."

So Laban gave a great feast in honour of the wedding. But that night he brought his elder daughter to Jacob, pretending that she was Rachel. In the morning, when Jacob saw that he had married the wrong sister, he cried out, "What have you done? It was Rachel I worked for all these years, not Leah."

"In our country," Laban replied, "it is not proper for the younger daughter to be married before the elder. I will give Rachel to you as your second wife if you will work for me another seven years."

So Rachel became Jacob's wife too, and he loved her more than ever. But he still had to work another seven years for his uncle.

He worked hard and grew rich, and his wives gave him many sons. But Laban was jealous of Jacob's success and Jacob began to feel homesick. One night God appeared to him in a dream and said, "Go back to Canaan, to the land of your fathers. I will protect you."

So Jacob set off in secret with his wives and sons, his flocks and herds, to return to Canaan. But unknown to him, Rachel had taken the household gods—the precious images her father used when they worshipped together. When Laban found out that Jacob had gone, he rode after him and when he had caught up with him he asked angrily, "Why did you go without telling me, and why did you steal my gods?"

"I was afraid you would stop my wives from coming with me," Jacob replied. "But I did not steal your gods. You may search my camp."

Then Laban searched but found nothing, as Rachel had hidden the gods in her camel-bag and was sitting on it. Then Laban and Jacob made friends and Laban rode home.

Joseph's Coat of Many Colours

God had commanded Jacob to return to the land of Canaan, to farm it together with his sons. Jacob had twelve sons, but only two of them were the children of his best-loved wife, Rachel. The elder of the two, named Joseph, Jacob loved more than all his other children, but he loved the younger, whose name was Benjamin, almost as much.

By the time Joseph was seventeen his brothers had come to hate him because they were jealous of their father's great love for the boy. Their anger was increased when Joseph showed them a coat Jacob had given him. It was made in many colours and had sleeves of the kind that princes wore. "Our father spoils the boy," they thought to themselves.

One night, Joseph had a dream, and in the morning he told it to his brothers. "I dreamed that we were all out in the fields binding up the sheaves, and my sheaf rose on its end and stood upright, while your sheaves gathered round it and bowed down to the ground."

"What!" said his brothers. "Do you think that you will be king some day and rule over us?" And they hated him even more than before.

Joseph had another dream, and this he told to his father as well as his brothers. "In my dream," he said, "the sun and the moon and eleven stars were all bowing down before me."

Even his father grew angry with him then. "What is this dream of yours?" he said. "Must we all come and bow low before you, I and your mother and your brothers, just as if you were a king?"

After this Joseph's brothers grew even more savagely jealous and hated what they thought was his pride. But his father did not forget the dream.

One day, as the brothers were minding their father's sheep on the plains, Jacob sent Joseph out to look for them and to tell him whether everything was all right. Joseph set out in search of them, and a man he met told him where their flocks were grazing.

The brothers saw Joseph a long way off and recognized him by his robe. "Here comes the dreamer," they said. "Now is our chance to kill him, for we are alone and no one will ever know. We can throw his body into this deep pit and say that a wild beast has eaten him."

But Reuben, the eldest of the brothers, felt sorry for Joseph, and persuaded the others to spare his life. They agreed instead to beat him and throw him into the pit, hoping he would die of exposure. But Reuben intended to come back on his own

to rescue Joseph.

So when Joseph came up to his brothers expecting to be welcomed, they turned on him instead and beat him cruelly. Then they stripped off his robe and threw him into the nearby pit.

Then they sat down to eat, and while they were resting they saw a caravan in the distance, carrying spices southwards to Egypt. Then Judah said, "I have an idea. Why don't we sell our brother to these merchants, instead of leaving him to die in this pit?"

So Joseph was pulled up out of the pit and sold to the merchants for twenty pieces of silver. They took Joseph with them to Egypt, and sold him there as a slave.

When Reuben came back to the pit to rescue Joseph he found it empty. "The boy is lost," he cried out in distress. "Now how can I take him back to our father?" And he tore his clothes in sorrow.

Meanwhile, the others had killed a goat, and then taken Joseph's robe and dipped it in the goat's blood. They slashed the robe to bits, as if a wild beast had savaged it, and brought it to their father. "Look what we have found!" they cried. "Do you recognize it? Isn't this Joseph's robe?"

"Yes," Jacob replied sadly, "it *is* Joseph's robe. A wild beast has attacked him and torn him to pieces." And he wept and tore his clothes in sorrow for the son he had loved so well. His other children tried to comfort him, but it was useless. "I will go on mourning Joseph's death until the day I die," he said.

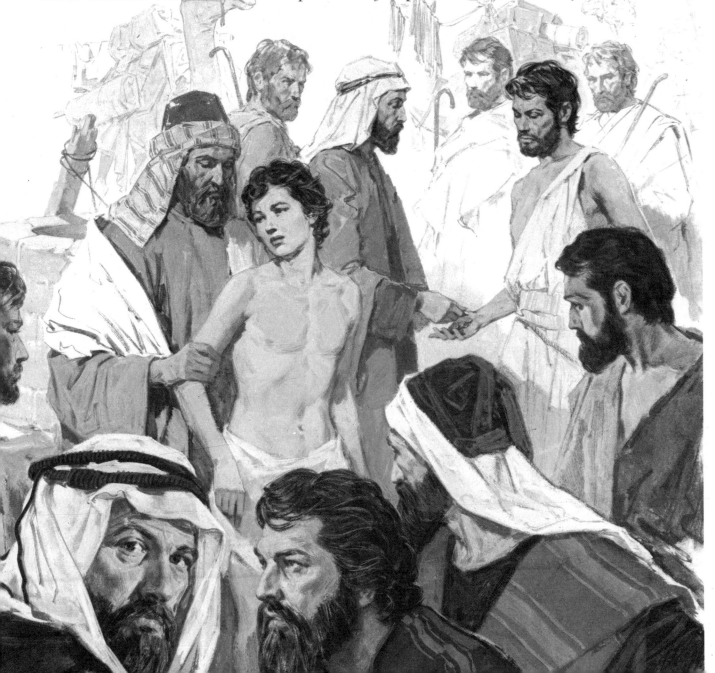

Pharaoh's Dreams

JOSEPH, now a slave in Egypt, was unjustly put in prison. There he interpreted the dreams of Pharaoh's chief butler and baker. The chief butler, about to be freed, promised to plead to Pharaoh for Joseph's release. But two years passed and still Joseph remained locked up.

Then one night Pharaoh had a dream: he was standing by the river Nile, when suddenly seven sleek, fat cows came up out of the river and started grazing on the land. Next Pharaoh saw seven more cows, looking very thin and scraggy, come up out of the river and stand among the seven fat cows. Then the thin cows started to fight the fat

ones and ate them all up. The dream faded away and Pharaoh awoke, deeply troubled.

Then he had a second dream: seven full and ripe ears of wheat were growing on one stalk, and immediately behind them were seven more ears of wheat, empty and shrivelled up by the wind. The empty ears seemed to swallow up the full ones, and again Pharaoh awoke and was afraid.

When morning came, he called together all the magicians and wise men of Egypt. He told them about his dreams, but not one of them could tell him what they meant. Then Pharaoh's chief butler suddenly remembered about Joseph, and he told Pharaoh how

Joseph had interpreted their dreams when he and the chief baker had been in prison, and how he had quite correctly predicted life for one of them and death for the other.

Pharaoh was impressed by this and sent for Joseph at once. He was brought out of the Round Tower and taken to court. When he had listened to Pharaoh's dream, he said:

"These two dreams are really one dream. God has told Pharaoh what he intends to do. The seven fat cows represent seven years, and the seven full ears of wheat mean the same seven years—these will be years of plenty. The seven thin cows also mean seven years, and the empty ears of wheat are those same seven years—and these years will be years of famine. This means that there will be seven years of good harvests and of great wealth, and then there will be seven years of drought and famine when nothing will grow and your animals will starve, and the whole land of Egypt will lie in ruins.

"Because God's will is set on this, it would be as well for you to lay in stores against these years of famine by appointing overseers and marshals in every part of the land to gather and store one fifth of every crop to feed you in the poor years. You must build new granaries and storehouses and they must be well guarded. This is the only way you will have enough food for the people during these years of famine. Only in this way can you save Egypt."

Pharaoh was amazed at the way Joseph interpreted his dreams, and also at the wise advice he gave. He said to Joseph:

"Since it is God who has made these things known to you, you are obviously possessed of unusually great wisdom and powers beyond those of other men. I appoint you to be in charge of my household, and all my people will do as you command. I hereby give you authority and power over the whole of Egypt."

Pharaoh took off his royal signet ring and put it on Joseph's finger to show that he was to be his viceroy. Then he sent for fine clothes for Joseph to wear and hung a golden chain of office around his neck. He gave him his viceroy's chariot to travel about in, and men would cry, "Make way!" when they saw him coming. Pharaoh also gave Joseph an Egyptian woman to be his wife, and a new Egyptian name.

Then God sent the Egyptian people seven years of rich and fruitful harvests, and Joseph had the grain gathered and stored in the cities. Great granaries were specially built to house it, until the grain was piled far and wide like the sand on the seashore—beyond all counting.

When the seven years of plenty had ended they were followed, as Joseph had foretold, by seven years of famine. There was famine in every country of the world, but Egypt alone was prepared for it and had enough grain in store to feed its people. And before the famine had ended people from all over the world had come to Joseph in Egypt, to buy wheat from him.

Joseph's Brothers in Egypt

WHEN Jacob heard that there was wheat to be bought in Egypt while the rest of the world was starving, he said to his sons, "Go to Egypt and buy some of this wheat and bring it back here so that we can all eat bread again."

Then Jacob's sons saddled their mules and set out for Egypt. They left their youngest brother, Benjamin, behind, for he was their father's favourite now that Joseph had gone, and Jacob was afraid that some harm might befall him on the way.

When Jacob's sons arrived in Egypt they presented themselves to Joseph, as the

governor of the land, and bowed low before him and asked for wheat. Joseph recognized his brothers at once, but he pretended not to know them, and spoke harshly to them. "Where are you from?" he asked. "From Canaan," they replied. "We have come to buy food."

They did not recognize Joseph at all, for they did not expect to see their brother ever again, and certainly not as Pharaoh's right-hand man, the most important man in Egypt.

"You are spies," Joseph said to them. "You have come to spy out Egypt's defences, and you must be punished."

"No, no, sir," his brothers protested, "we are not spies, we have just come to buy food. We are honest men, sir, twelve brothers from Canaan. The youngest has remained at home with our father, and the other has disappeared."

Now Joseph specially longed to see Benjamin again, for he was the youngest, and Rachel's only other son besides Joseph himself.

So he said to his brothers, "I will find out if you are telling the truth. Leave one of your brothers behind with me, take the food you need for your people, and go. If you bring your youngest brother back with you I shall know you are not spies, but honest men. Then I will let your other brother go, and you can all return home freely."

Then he took his brother Simeon as the hostage, and filled their sacks up with wheat, and they all went back to their father Jacob in Canaan.

Jacob did not want to lose Benjamin and he forbade the others to take him to Egypt. But soon the famine grew so bad that there was no food at all left in Canaan, and they were once again forced to go to Egypt to buy some. This time they took Benjamin with them, and Jacob sent gifts of balsam and honey, myrrh and almonds, to the governor of Egypt, hoping to soften his heart towards his sons.

When Joseph saw that his brothers had brought Benjamin he was overjoyed and ordered a great feast to be prepared. "Is your father still alive?" he asked them. "Is he well?" "Yes, sir," they answered, "he is alive and well."

Then Joseph was overcome with tears, and he went and hid himself so they would not see him crying. But it was not the proper time for him to reveal himself as their brother, so he swallowed his tears and came back to them, and ordered the feast to be served.

When it was over Joseph had his brothers' sacks filled with wheat, and in Benjamin's sack he hid his own silver goblet underneath the grain.

At daybreak the next day the brothers left to start their journey, but before they had gone more than a few miles Joseph sent his steward after them, to accuse them of stealing his goblet. The steward searched their sacks, and of course the goblet was found in Benjamin's. The brothers insisted they knew nothing about it, and begged the steward to let their youngest brother go free.

"You'll have to ask my master about that," said the steward. So they all returned to the city to beg the Egyptian governor for mercy for Benjamin.

But Joseph said, "Because my goblet was found on him he must become my slave, but the rest of you may go free."

Then Judah came up to him and said, "Please listen, sir. You are as powerful as Pharaoh, so we beg you to understand our distress. If we leave our brother Benjamin here, our father, who is very old, will surely die of sorrow, for he will have lost the two sons he loved best. I beg you, let me take the boy's place here, and let him go free."

Joseph could contain himself no longer. He sent all his attendants away and said to them, "I am your brother Joseph, the brother you sold to the merchants. With God's help I have become great; I have saved men's lives and now I have saved yours too, for the sake of your descendants. Go back to our father in Canaan and tell him that the famine will go on for another five years. Bring him back with you to Egypt, and bring your flocks and your herds and everything you own. And hurry!"

Then he threw his arms around Benjamin and hugged him, and kissed each of his brothers, in turn and wept for joy.

The Famine

THE famine raged in every country; both Egypt and Canaan suffered terribly. Joseph, as governor of the land, collected all the silver in Egypt and in Canaan in exchange for the wheat which the people bought, and stored it in Pharaoh's treasury. When all the silver in Egypt and in Canaan had been collected and taken away, the Egyptians said to Joseph, "Give us bread or we shall die. We have no more silver to buy wheat."

Joseph said, "If your silver is all gone, you can bring me your herds and I will give you bread in exchange." So the people brought their herds to Joseph and he gave them bread. For a whole year the people were able to feed off the bread they had exchanged for their livestock. But still the famine went on raging, and finally the people came back to Joseph and said:

"My lord, our silver and our cattle now all belong to Pharaoh, and we have nothing left but our bodies and our land. Take us and the land we live on in payment for bread, and we will serve Pharaoh in bondage. For if we have no food we shall die, and if we die there will be no one to farm our land

and it will become desert once again."

So Joseph bought up all the land in Egypt for Pharaoh, and he set the people working as slaves from one end of the land to the other. He gave them seed so that they could plant new crops, and he made them give one fifth of every crop to Pharaoh.

At last the time came when Joseph's father Jacob was nearing his death. His sons all gathered round his bed to receive his last blessing. Joseph had brought his two sons, Manasseh and Ephraim, who had been born to him in Egypt. "These are my sons, the gift of God," he said to his father. Then Jacob held the boys close to him and kissed them and said, "I had not expected ever to see my son's face again, and now God has allowed me to see his sons as well." And he blessed them in turn. Then he blessed each one of his own twelve sons and foretold that they would be the founders of the twelve tribes of Israel.

"When I am dead," he said to them, "don't leave my body in Egypt. Bury me in Canaan with my forefathers." And with these words he died.

Pharaoh ordered a period of mourning for Jacob all over Egypt, lasting for 70 days. All the leaders of Egypt followed Joseph and his brothers as they went to bury Jacob in Canaan, in the land which God had given to him and his descendants for ever.

Moses in the Bulrushes

PHARAOH invited Jacob's twelve sons to come and live in Egypt. They worked hard as the years went by, and their families grew large enough to be known as tribes and settled all over Egypt. They were known as Israelites, from the name God had given Jacob long before.

But they were not happy people. They still lived in Goshen, the fertile district that had been given to them by the friendly Pharaoh who had invited their forefathers to come to Egypt. But now the Egyptians made them work hard, clearing the land and digging channels through the fields so that the crops could get water from the Nile. They were made to bake bricks, too, for a great new city was being built.

A new Pharaoh had come to the throne, who remembered nothing about Joseph. "These Israelites outnumber us," he told the Egyptians, "and they are more powerful than we are. We must protect ourselves against them, for if a war breaks out they will join our enemies, and take over our country."

So Pharaoh made slaves of the Israelites, and tried to break their spirit with hard work. But it seemed that the worse they were treated the more children they had. Their tribes grew larger and larger, and the Egyptians feared and hated them even more.

Then Pharaoh sent for the Hebrew midwives and said, "When you are helping the Hebrew women give birth, watch if the child is a boy or a girl. If it is a girl, let her live, but if it is a boy, kill him instantly."

The midwives knew Pharaoh was asking them to do wrong, so they let the boys live. Then Pharaoh ordered his own people to drown every newborn Hebrew boy in the Nile.

One woman, though, a descendant of Jacob's son Levi, gave birth to a fine boy, and managed to hide him from the Egyptians. When the baby was three months old the Levite woman could not hide him any longer. She bought a basket woven of rushes and made it watertight with clay and tar. Then she laid the baby in it and hid the basket in the reeds of the river bank. She went home in tears, but her daughter waited nearby to see what would happen.

Presently Pharaoh's daughter came down to bathe in the Nile. She noticed the basket hidden in the reeds and sent a servant to fetch it. When she opened it, the baby was crying and at once she felt sorry for it. "Why," she said, "it is a Hebrew baby someone has left to die."

At that moment the boy's sister ran up. "Shall I fetch a Hebrew woman who can nurse the baby for you?" she asked. Pharaoh's daughter wanted to keep the child, so she sent the girl to find a nurse. The girl ran and fetched the baby's own mother.

"Here is a child I have found," the princess said to her. "I want you to nurse him and take care of him for me." The woman did not tell the princess who she was—she was too happy at having saved her baby's life. So she took her child and looked after him until he was old enough to serve Pharaoh's daughter. When the Egyptian princess saw the boy she was so pleased with him that she adopted him as her own son. She called him Moses because the name meant that he was someone who had been drawn out of the water.

The Voice from the Burning Bush

MOSES grew up in the household of Pharaoh's daughter, but he knew he was an Israelite by birth. One day he killed an Egyptian who was ill-treating an Israelite slave, and fled to the land of Midian. Here he married the daughter of Jethro, a village priest.

One day, as he was leading his father-in-law's flocks beside the desert to graze in wild pastures, he came to Horeb, the mountain sacred to God, and he saw an extraordinary thing. A bush on the mountainside was burning, but although the flames came from it, the bush itself was not burned.

As Moses stood there marvelling, the voice of God called to him out of the fire, "Moses, Moses," and he replied, "Here I am."

"Don't come any closer," God said to him, "and take your shoes off, for you are standing on holy ground. I am the God of Abraham, the God of Isaac, and the God of Jacob." And Moses did as God told him, but he covered up his face, for he was afraid to look directly at God.

Then God said, "I have seen the sufferings of my people in Egypt; I have heard them crying out to me, and now I have come to rescue them from the Egyptians and bring them to the good and fruitful land where the Canaanites and the Hittites live. Come—I will send you to Pharaoh, and you shall bring the children of Israel safely out of Egypt."

Moses was afraid. He said to God, "Who am I, to be given so much responsibility?"

"Don't be afraid," God said to him, "I will help you, and to prove that I have sent you, when you have brought your people safely out of Egypt, you will all come here to this mountain to worship me."

Then Moses said, "If I go and tell the Israelites that the God of their forefathers has sent me, they will ask me his name, and then what shall I say?"

God answered, "Tell them that God has sent you, their God Jehovah, the God of their fathers Abraham and Isaac and Jacob, for this is my name for ever."

But Moses still said, "I don't think they will believe me."

"What is that in your hand?" God asked him.

"A staff of wood," he replied.

God said, "Throw it on the ground," and Moses did so, and at once it became a wriggling snake. He jumped back in horror, but God said, "Pick it up by the tail." Trembling, Moses did, and it turned back into a staff again.

Then God said, "Put your hand inside your cloak," and Moses did. When he drew his hand out again, it was all white and covered with sores. Then God told him to do it again, and when he pulled his hand out, God had healed it completely.

God said to Moses, "I am giving you these signs to prove to the people that you are my messenger and that I, and I alone, have sent you to help and guide them."

The Plagues of Egypt

M OSES asked Pharaoh to free the Israelites, but Pharaoh refused. Then God said to Moses, "Pharaoh will not allow my people to go. Go and strike the river Nile with your staff, and the water in all Egypt's rivers and wells will be changed into blood. The fish will die and the rivers will stink, and the Egyptians won't be able to drink the water. There will be blood all through the land of Egypt–I will show Pharaoh that I am God."

Moses did as God commanded, but still Pharaoh would not set the Israelites free.

Then God said to Moses, "Go again to Pharaoh and say, 'Let my people go. If you refuse, I will plague your land with frogs.

They will come up from the rivers into your house, into your bed, into your ovens and into your bread. They will climb all over you and your people.'" And the frogs swarmed all over the land. But still Pharaoh would not set the people free.

God said to Moses, "Stretch out your staff and strike the dust on the ground, and the dust will fly up and change into mosquitoes. These will sting every animal and every Egyptian in the land." When Pharaoh saw the plague of mosquitoes, he said to his magicians, "Surely your magic is as good as the Hebrews'? Get rid of these mosquitoes !." But the magicians were frightened. "This is no ordinary magic," they said to

Pharaoh, "God has done this to the Egyptians." But still Pharaoh would not listen to them.

"Let my people go," Moses said to Pharaoh. "If you don't, God will send down swarms of flies. Your houses will be filled with them, but not the houses of *my* people." The air over Egypt was filled with flies – but still Pharaoh would not let the Israelites go.

Then God struck the herds of Egypt down with a sickness so bad that most of the beasts died. He sent a fine dust over the land, and the dust settled on men and animals alike and turned into boils and sores that festered on their bodies. But still Pharaoh would not listen.

Then God sent a great hailstorm with hail the size of rocks; the hail killed every man and beast that was out in the open fields – but still Pharaoh would not listen.

Then God said to Moses, "Stretch out your staff and locusts will come and eat up what few crops the hail has left," and Moses did so, and such swarms of locusts descended on Egypt that the whole land was black with them. They ate until there was nothing green left throughout the land.

Then God said to Moses, "Stretch out your staff towards the sky, and there will be darkness over the land." The darkness that came was so heavy that it could be felt, and for three days there was no light at all.

Then at last Pharaoh was prepared to let the Israelites go, but he said they must leave their herds behind. "No," Moses said to him, "God has spared our animals because we need them to support ourselves and to sacrifice to him. Our flocks and herds must go with us."

Then Pharaoh was furious. "Get out and never let me see you again," he said to Moses. "I will never let your people go."

41

The Night of the Passover

THEN God sent Moses to warn Pharaoh. "At midnight tonight," Moses told him, "the God of Israel will go out among the Egyptians, and every first-born creature in the land will die—the eldest son of Pharaoh himself and the eldest son of the slave at the mill and the first-born of every animal in the fields.

"The whole land of Egypt will cry out in dreadful anguish, a cry of sorrow more terrible than any that has ever been heard, or will ever be heard again. But not one man or beast belonging to the Israelites will be hurt – not even one dog's tongue will be so much as scratched."

But Pharaoh still would not set the people free.

Then God gave Moses instructions for the Israelites, and he called all the elders of his people together and gave them God's commands:

"Each man must take a sheep or a kid for his household and kill it and prepare it as a sacrifice to our God. Then take a bunch of marjoram, dip it into the blood and smear blood onto the lintel of each door and on the two doorposts. Nobody must use the door of his house until morning, for tonight God will go through the land of Egypt and kill every first-born son, but when he sees the mark on each door he will pass over it and will do no harm to anyone inside that house."

The people of Israel listened to Moses. They kneeled down and worshipped God, then they hurried away to do as God had commanded them.

By midnight that night God had struck down every first-born in Egypt, from Pharaoh's own son in the palace to the first-born of the captive in his prison.

Before the night was over a terrible cry of anguish and mourning was heard all over Egypt, because death had come to every single family in the land.

While it was still dark Pharaoh sent for Moses and Aaron. "Get up and go," he cried. "Serve your God and let us alone. Take your sheep and your cattle and leave my land for ever—and as you go, remember

to ask your God to send me his blessing instead of this dreadful curse."

The Egyptians urged the Israelites to hurry because they wanted to get rid of them before anything worse happened. The Israelites hurried to leave in case Pharaoh might change his mind. They snatched up their belongings, and because their bread dough had not had time to rise, they wrapped up the basins with the dough in them inside their cloaks, just as they were. Then they left Egypt for ever.

The Crossing of the Red Sea

When Pharaoh heard that all the 600,000 Israelites had gone off with their families and their cattle, he regretted letting them go. He hardly had any slaves left to do the work. He ordered every war chariot in Egypt to be made ready and galloped after the Israelites, taking with him all the regiments of his cavalry and his infantry. It was a mighty army and the thunder of the horses' hooves and the rumble of the chariot wheels could be heard a long way off.

ONCE the Israelites had left Egypt they rested and made fires on which to bake their bread. They baked the dough just as it was, kneaded flat, because there was no time to let it rise. In later times men and women would be proud to eat this unleavened bread in memory of the Israelites fleeing through the desert to freedom.

Moses did not take the people back to Canaan by the shortest way, because that would have meant crossing through the land of the Philistines. The Israelites, weak after their long years of captivity, were no match for that fierce tribe. The Philistines would have killed them and driven off their flocks and herds in triumph.

"I will protect my chosen people from danger," said God, "and guide them safely through places where no man lives."

As they marched, a cloud of smoke went ahead of them showing the way, and at night it was a cloud of fire that reached up into the sky.

By these signs God guided the Israelites through the wilderness to the shore of the Red Sea. Here the cloud stood still, and they camped because God commanded it.

44

From their camp by the Red Sea the Israelites saw the great army of Egyptians appear in the distance.

"Help us, Lord!" they cried out in terror. Then they turned on Moses.

"Why did you take us out of Egypt to die like this?" they complained. "We would have been better off living as slaves."

Then God said to Moses, "Tell your people not to be afraid. They must pick up all their possessions and follow you. Raise your staff in front of you, and stretch it out over the sea, and I promise that the waters will part in two and you will be able to walk on dry land right across the sea bed. When you are all safely across, I will fill the Egyptians' hearts with hatred of you. They will rush after you, and then I shall destroy them."

Then the cloud of smoke that was God's signal moved from in front of the Israelites to behind them, so that it lay between them

were escaping from them, they rushed after them into the sea, with their horses and chariots, their infantry and cavalry. But their chariot wheels sank in the wet sand, and the horses and men were bogged down.

"God himself is fighting for Israel!" the Egyptians cried. They looked around them and what they saw filled them with terror. They were trapped between the two great walls of water.

Panic broke out. Soldiers threw down their weapons and tried to run for their lives. But their feet sank deeper and deeper into the sand. The horses reared in the chariot shafts, whinnying and pounding the air.

The commanders made one last effort. They ordered the men to return to their chariots and wrench the wheels free.

But it was no use. They could move neither forwards nor backwards; they were all stuck fast in the middle of the Red Sea.

Then God commanded Moses to stretch out his staff over the sea again, and the walls of water gave way. With a mighty roar the sea water swept over Pharaoh's army, over his chariots and over his horses, so that every man and beast was drowned.

When the Israelites saw such a great army destroyed, and all the bodies piled along the shore, they feared their God more than ever, and respected Moses his servant, too, for they knew that it was God who had saved the children of Israel from the power of Pharaoh.

Then Miriam, the sister of Moses and of Aaron, picked up her tambourine and began a dance of joy. And all the women followed her, dancing to the sound of their tambourines and singing:

"Sing to the Lord for he is triumphant;
  The horse and his rider are thrown into the sea.
  Sing to the Lord for he is my refuge;
  My God and my strength he shall always be."

and the Egyptians, hiding them from the Egyptians so that they could not see what was happening.

Moses stretched out his staff towards the sea, and a strong wind started to blow. It blew all night, so hard that it pushed back the sea water and made the sea bed into dry land. The Israelites were able to walk across on the sea bed, with high walls of water on either side of them.

When the Egyptians saw the Israelites

The Ten Commandments

IT was now nearly three months since the Israelites had left Egypt. They had been travelling through the wilderness of Sinai, and by the time they reached the foot of Mount Sinai they were tired.

Moses told them to pitch their tents in the plain beneath the mountain, and while they made their camp and gathered brushwood to build fires, he himself climbed up the slopes to the mountaintop. There the voice of God spoke to him and said:

"At this place, on this mountain, I will begin to make the Israelites into my chosen people. I have brought them safely out of Egypt where they were Pharaoh's slaves. Now I will give them, through you, laws and commandments that will rule them every day of their lives. They must obey me from the day they are born until the day they die. If they do all that I tell them to do, I will make them into a holy nation, for they are the people I have chosen to be my special possession. Go now, and tell this to your people."

Moses came back down the mountain to the plains below. He called the elders, who were the leaders of the people, together, and told them what God had said.

"Whatever God has said, we will do," the people cried out, and Moses climbed back up the mountain, and again found himself in the presence of God.

"Go, then," God told Moses when he had heard what the people said, "go back to the people and tell them to prepare themselves for what is to come. Tell them to purify themselves, to wash themselves and their clothes, and to clear their thoughts for two days. On the third day I will come down onto Mount Sinai and speak to them. But not one of them must go near the mountain in the meantime."

The people did as Moses told them, waiting eagerly for the days to pass. They built a barrier around the mountain, to show that its slopes were holy ground.

On the morning of the third day there was a storm with thunder and lightning, and a dark cloud covered Mount Sinai. Suddenly a trumpet sounded, so loudly that it seemed to fill the air, and the people in the camp beneath the mountain trembled with fear.

Moses led the people out to the foot of Mount Sinai, and the sound of the trumpet grew louder and louder around them. Then God came down like a fire onto Sinai, and the whole top of the mountain was wrapped in dense clouds of smoke as if it were a volcano erupting.

Then Moses spoke to God. The Israelites standing around him heard God's answers as a peal of thunder so loud that it hurt their ears, and they threw themselves to the earth in terror.

But Moses heard God calling him to climb the mountain yet again and talk to him. The watching Israelites saw their leader climb upwards, higher and higher, until he disappeared into the smoke that covered the mountaintop, and they trembled.

These are the rules God gave Moses for the Israelites to follow. They are known as the Ten Commandments.

"I am the Lord your God: you must have no other god, but me.

"You must not worship anything you have made yourselves, nor must you worship statues or pictures or images of anything that is in the sky or in the earth or beneath the earth. I am your God and I say that you must worship the being that is me, and only me. If you break this commandment I shall punish not just you but your children and your children's children. But I shall always be kind and merciful to the people who love me and obey my commandments.

"You must not call on the name of God without good reason, nor use it wrongly or without respect.

"Remember to keep the seventh day holy. On six days you can work and do all that you have to do, but the seventh day is my Sabbath. On this day you must not work, nor must any member of your family, or your household, or your animals, or even the stranger staying in your house. For in six days I made the heavens and the earth and the sea and all that is in them, and on the seventh day I rested. So I blessed the seventh day and made it a day of rest for ever.

"Respect and honour your father and your mother.

"You must not murder another human being.

"You must not sleep with another man's wife.

"You must not steal.

"You must not tell lies nor must you give evidence that is false.

"You must not long for anyone else's possessions and wish that you owned them yourself – do not envy another man's house, nor his wife, nor his servant, nor his cow, nor his donkey, nor anything else he has.

Remember, it is his, not yours."

Then God gave Moses more laws to guide the people in their daily lives. He said:

"You must love the Lord your God with all your heart and with all your soul and with all your strength. Teach your children to love me as you do, and I will reward you.

"And if any kind of hurt is done to you, you must pay back a life for a life, an eye for an eye, a tooth for a tooth, a hand for a hand, a burn for a burn, and a wound for a wound.

"Do not let yourself be led into doing something you know to be wrong because the majority of people favour it.

"Do not be unkind to anyone who is a stranger among you. Remember how you yourselves felt when you were strangers in Egypt.

"Sow your land and harvest the crops for six years running, but the seventh year let the land lie fallow and rest, so that it will be richer when you come to sow it again.

"Every first-born thing belongs to me. This applies to the males of all your herds and flocks, and to your first-born sons too. You must offer each first-born to me, and then buy it back again. Be sure never to come into my presence without an offering in your hands."

At last the watching people saw Moses coming back down the mountainside. They gathered around him to hear what God had said. But Moses spent a long time in his tent writing down all the commandments God had given him. Then he built an altar at the foot of Mount Sinai, and ordered bulls to be killed as sacrifices to God. Some of their blood he poured into basins and set on the altar; some he poured on the stones of the altar itself. Then Moses read God's commandments so that everyone could hear.

"We will do exactly as God has ordered us," the people shouted joyfully.

The Making of the Golden Calf

Moses' climbed the mountain again and for forty days and nights God told him how to make the Ark—a holy place in which to keep the Commandments.

But when Moses was so long coming down, the leaders of the Israelites gathered around his brother Aaron and said:

"This man Moses who brought us out of Egypt seems to have disappeared and we don't know what has become of him. We need a new god to lead us."

Aaron told them to take the gold ornaments that their women wore and bring them to him. The people stripped themselves of their earrings and necklaces and Aaron took their gold and melted it down over a fire. Then he moulded the gold into the shape of a bull calf, and told the Israelites to worship it.

Aaron had no sooner done this than he grew afraid at what he had done, so he built an altar in front of the calf, and told the people that they must spend the next day worshipping God.

Next morning the people got up early and offered sacrifices before the calf, and worshipped it. Then they began to eat and drink. Before long the whole camp was filled with people dancing and singing and feasting.

Up on the mountain God said to Moses, "Go down at once – your people have done a shameful thing. They have forgotten my commandments and have made themselves a statue of a bull calf. They are kneeling in front of it and making sacrifices, and calling it their god. I shall punish them for this – I shall destroy them all."

"Don't destroy them, Lord," Moses pleaded with him. "Don't be so angry with your own chosen people, whom you took so much trouble to save from Pharaoh. Have mercy – remember Abraham and Isaac and Jacob, and the promise you made them that their children should be as countless as the stars in heaven, and how you promised them their own land for all time."

God listened to Moses, and decided to spare the Israelites after all.

Moses came down from the mountain, carrying the two stone tablets on which God had written all his commandments to the Israelites. Joshua, who was with him, said, "Listen – do you hear all that noise coming from the camp? The people must surely be at war."

"That's not the sound of fighting," Moses replied, "It's the sound of singing and feasting."

When they drew near to the camp they saw the golden calf and the dancing, and Moses was angry – so angry that he flung the tablets down, and they were shattered to pieces at the foot of the mountain. Then he seized the calf and made a great fire and burned it. When the fire had died away Moses took the last remnants of the calf from the fire and ground them to dust. He threw the dust into water and made the people drink it as a punishment.

Moses spoke harshly to Aaron too, but he could see that Aaron was not really able to control the people if he himself was not there. It was on Moses that all the responsibility of leadership always had to rest.

The Story of Samson

SOMETIMES God chose the least likely men and women to work for him. There was Samson—a rough, wild man with a short temper—who was for ever getting into trouble with his own people, the Israelites, and his enemies, the Philistines.

But he had been marked out by God from the start. Before he was born his mother was visited by an angel.

"You shall have a son," he had said to her, "who will belong to God. He will be marked out from other people by his hair. It will make him as strong as a lion, and for that reason it must never be cut."

God's words came true. The baby was born and the woman named him Samson. He grew into a fine young man, larger and

stronger than any around him, and his parents were very proud of him. One day, he told his parents he wanted to marry a Philistine girl whom he had seen in the neighbouring town of Timnath. They were not pleased because the Philistines were their enemies, but Samson insisted.

As he was walking through the vineyards on his way to Timnath, he was attacked by a lion. He had no weapon, but God gave him the strength to kill the lion with his bare hands. He left the carcass lying there and went on to visit the girl. The marriage was arranged to take place in a few weeks.

At the wedding feast Samson boasted that he would set the guests a riddle that none of them could answer.

"Out of the eater came something to eat,
Out of the strong came something sweet,"
he said. (On the way to the feast he had seen that bees had made a nest inside the carcass of the lion he had killed, and built a honeycomb.)

The guests could not answer the riddle. In the end, tired of guessing, they persuaded his bride to ask him what the answer was. He told her, and in no time at all the girl had disclosed it to the Philistines. They came back to him, shouting:

"What is sweeter than honey?
What is stronger than a lion?"

Samson was so angry at what his wife had done that he killed 30 young men and burned the Philistines' crops in revenge. They in turn killed the treacherous bride and her

father. Ill feeling between the two tribes had reached a peak.

Then one day Samson disappeared and went to live high up in the mountains, in a cave. The Philistines turned on Samson's people and gave them more trouble than ever before. In the end, in return for peace, they forced the people to say where Samson was hiding, and to bring him down from the mountains, tied up with ropes.

When Samson came face to face with his enemies again his old anger returned. He strained at the ropes that held him down, and they snapped like gut strings. He looked around for some weapon, and snatched up the jawbone from a dead donkey lying beside the road. With it he attacked the Philistines so fiercely that 1,000 men fell dead under his blows, and the rest fled in terror. Still Samson's enemies were determined to capture him. The Philistines knew that they would never catch him by force, for he was stronger than any man. He could tear down doors and break through chains. His strength had been given him by God, and it was this secret power that the Philistines were determined to break.

They went to a beautiful woman named Delilah, and told her to spy on him.

"Find out by what magic means he remains so strong," they said. "If you can make him weak like other men, we will give you 1,100 pieces of silver."

It did not take Delilah long to make Samson come and see her. It took her even less long to make him fall in love with her, and to promise to give her whatever she asked for.

"Tell me the secret of your great strength, Samson," she asked.

"Tie me up with new bow strings, and I will grow weak like other men," he said. So Delilah waited until he was asleep and then tied him up with the strings.

"The Philistines are attacking you, Sam-son!" she cried.

Samson awoke instantly and freed himself with one quick wrench. Then he stood there laughing at Delilah for pretending to capture him.

She asked him again, "Tell me the secret of your strength, Samson." "Tie me up with new rope, and I will grow weak like other men," he said.

Again she waited until he was asleep, and again she tied him up. "The Philistines are attacking you!" she cried. Samson woke, and broke through the rope as if it had been a thread.

At last he told her the truth. "I am one of the people chosen by God," he said. "My strength lies in my hair; it must never be cut. If it is, I will become as weak as other men."

Delilah drugged his wine and cradled him to sleep on her lap. Then she cut off his hair. She called in the Philistines and they bound him and blinded him and threw him into prison. They paid Delilah the silver.

Samson was put to work like an animal, grinding grain. Now that he was blind and weak, the Philistines decided to put him on show to the public in the temple. The people crowded into the temple of their god, Dagon, celebrating Samson's downfall. When they saw their old enemy they jeered. "O Lord," Samson prayed to God, "give me back just once more the strength I used to have."

God guided him to the two central pillars that supported the temple. Samson took hold of one pillar with his right arm, and the other with his left. "Let me die with the Philistines," he prayed, and then he heaved at the pillars with all his strength.

The pillars cracked, then they broke, and with a roar like that of an earthquake the whole temple collapsed, burying everyone in it under a heap of stones. The people who mocked Samson were killed, and so was he.

Ruth and Boaz

NAOMI and her daughter-in-law, Ruth, had lived in the same house since they had both been widowed.

It was harvest time in Bethlehem.

"Go and pick up grain in the field that belongs to Boaz," Naomi said to Ruth. "He was related to my dead husband, and he is a kind man and will let you glean the wheat his reapers have left."

across the fields, cutting the wheat with sickles and tying the stalks into sheaves. Behind them followed the gleaners – women like Ruth who collected the stray ears of wheat the reapers dropped. It was back-breaking work, for they had to bend low to see the husks of wheat lying on the ground,

and it would take them all day to fill a small sack. But in this way people who had no fields of their own could get enough wheat to grind into flour and make bread for their families.

As the sun rose higher in the sky Boaz came out into the field, and watched the harvesters at work. He greeted them.

"The Lord be with you," he said, and they replied, "The Lord bless you." Then he noticed Ruth among the gleaners.

"Who is that girl?" he asked.

"She is a Moabite," his men replied. "She came here from her own country to be with the widow Naomi, your cousin. She has been on her feet since sunrise, gathering the

corn without stopping to rest at all."

Boaz called Ruth to him. "Stay in my field until the harvest is over," he said. She thanked him. "Stay and drink with us," Boaz went on. "I will see that no man bothers you. If you are thirsty, drink from my jars."

Ruth thanked him again and said, "Why are you so kind to me? I am a foreigner here." And Boaz replied:

"I have heard of your faithfulness and your love for Naomi. The God of Israel will bless you for it." Then he invited her to sit with him among the reapers and eat bread with him, and dip the bread in his wine. He gave her roasted grain to eat and she ate all she needed and saved the rest for Naomi. Boaz gave orders that she should be allowed to collect as much of his barley and wheat as she wished, even from among the sheaves.

The summer passed. The harvest had been gathered in, and the harvest festival had begun. Naomi said to her daughter-in-law:

"Tonight Boaz is threshing barley in his barn. He is my cousin, and, according to our laws, he can take you into his house as his wife. Go to him tonight; perhaps he will help you."

Ruth did as Naomi suggested, and Boaz greeted her joyfully, because he already loved her. He wanted to marry her, but he had to ask a cousin more closely related to the family than he was for permission. The cousin gave his consent and, as was customary, he showed his agreement by taking off his sandal and giving it to Boaz.

So Ruth became Boaz's wife and bore him a son. And Naomi's house was filled with children again by the daughter-in-law who loved her so dearly.

Samuel, Child of the Lord

THERE were two Israelite women married to the same husband: Peninnah, who had children, and Hannah, who had none. Every day Hannah would pray to God to give her a child, and every day Peninnah would mock her because he did not. When their husband, Elkanah, went to the temple of God to offer sacrifices, Hannah went with him to beg God for a son.

"Lord, please let me have a child," she prayed. "If you give me a son, then he shall be yours. I swear that I will bring him back to this temple, to serve you as one of your priests."

God heard her prayer. He gave her the son she longed for, and she called the boy Samuel. Much as she loved him, she remembered her promise. When he was not yet two years old, she went with Elkanah to the temple and brought Samuel to the priest, an old man called Eli. "This is my son whom God has given me," she said. "Now I am lending him back to God; his whole life shall be spent in God's service."

The boy Samuel grew up in the temple, where he was taught and cared for by Eli, who loved him like his own son.

One night, while Samuel was asleep, he heard a voice call, "Samuel, Samuel." He went to Eli and said, "Here I am."

"I did not call you," Eli replied.

Samuel went back to bed. But again the voice called, "Samuel, Samuel," and again he went to Eli. "Here I am," he said. "Surely you called me."

"I did not call you, my son," Eli replied. "Lie down again."

When Samuel was summoned for the third time Eli understood that it was God who was calling the child. "If he calls again," the priest said to Samuel, "you must say, 'Speak, Lord, your servant is listening.'"

Samuel went back to his place in the temple. "Samuel, Samuel!" the voice of God called once more, and this time Samuel replied, "Speak, Lord, your servant is listening."

Then the temple was filled with God's presence, and from that day on Samuel became God's prophet as Moses had been, and told the Israelites what God wanted them to do.

The years went by. The Israelites went to war with the Philistines again and the Philistine army won one battle after another. In desperation the Israelites sent men to fetch the Ark of the Covenant from God's temple, hoping that its presence would bring their army new strength. But God was angry with the Israelites for worshipping other gods, and allowed the battle to go against them.

The Philistines attacked so vigorously that they broke right through the Israelite lines and captured the sacred Ark. Demoralized, the Israelite army turned and fled.

When the old priest Eli heard that the Ark was captured, he was so distressed that he collapsed and died. Samuel was appointed Israel's leader and judge in his place.

The Ark did not stay long in the hands of the Philistines, however. They moved it from one city to another, but wherever it was kept the people fell sick and died, and the cities swarmed with rats.

So the Philistines returned the Ark to the Israelites, with rich gifts, and made peace with them. Samuel ruled Israel justly and the people worshipped God again.

David and Goliath

THE Philistines were on the move again. David was too young to fight in King Saul's army so he went on minding his father's sheep. But he longed to be a soldier like his three eldest brothers, who were fighting with the king.

David was sitting at table with his father Jesse, one day, when Jesse said to him:

"I want you to take this food to your brothers and then come back and tell me how they are."

David wasted no time. He found someone to look after the sheep in his place, and set off early the next morning. He reached King Saul's camp just as the two great armies were preparing themselves for the battle. The war cries of the Israelites, and the answering cries of their enemy, the Philistines, beat on his ears like fists on a drum.

There was no sign of his brothers in the rear column of soldiers, where David first looked. He pushed through the crowd of shouting soldiers until he found his brothers in the front line, near the king.

"What are you doing here?" Eliab, the eldest, cried when he saw David. "Go back at once; this is no place for a boy!"

Before David could reply there was a

sudden silence. From among the ranks of the Philistine army a giant, Goliath, had appeared.

"I challenge you, men of Israel," he roared. "If any one of you defeats me single-handed, we Philistines will be your slaves. If your man loses, we will take you all! Who among you is brave enough to fight me?"

"I am," shouted David.

The whole army of Israel turned to look at the boy, and his brothers said, "David, go home at once and mind your sheep."

David pushed his way forward to the king.

"Let me fight Goliath, sir," he begged, "and I will bring victory to Israel."

"You are a boy," the king said to him. "You cannot fight a giant like Goliath!"

"I am a shepherd," David replied. "When wild animals come and attack my father's flock I kill them. I have killed lions and bears, and I can kill Goliath–I know I can!"

"Go, then," said Saul, "and God be with you."

Saul put a bronze helmet on David's head and gave him a coat of mail to wear. Then he handed the boy his own sword.

David hesitated. "I cannot fight with these on," he said. "I must be free." He took off the king's armour again, and picked up his sling. Then he chose five smooth stones and put them in his shepherd's pouch.

The men around him fell back as he advanced, bare-handed, towards the giant Philistine, who stood towering above the armour bearer who carried his shield.

"I am ready," he said.

Goliath looked at his opponent. "You?" he said. "Who are you?" He fingered the sword he was carrying. A dagger hung from his belt, and he held a spear in his right hand. "I will take you and cut you up, and throw you to the sparrows as food," he said.

David moved forwards. "I am David, the son of Jesse," he said. "The men you see before you are soldiers of the army of our

Lord. Through our victory over the Philistines the world will know that our God is the true God, and that there is no other god than he. I am going to fight you and kill you, Goliath!"

With these words David raised his sling and aimed the stone in it at the giant. The stone flew through the air. It struck Goliath on the forehead, and the huge Philistine crashed to the ground. David ran to him and drew his sword out of its sheath. He held it high, and then sliced downwards, cutting off Goliath's head.

That was how the boy David became a hero in a day by killing the giant Goliath.

David and Absalom

IN all Israel there was no man more handsome than Absalom, the king's eldest son. His hair was thick and heavy, and when it was cut once in a year it weighed 200 shekels on the king's scales. David loved Absalom, and gave his son chariots and horses and warriors to serve him. But Absalom wanted more; he wanted his father's throne.

Every morning he would get up early and wait at the city gate. There he would stop any man who came to ask the king for a favour and question him about it. "You are certainly in the right," he would say, "but the king will not listen to you. If I were judge I would see that justice was done to everyone." The people used to come and fall down on their knees to him. But he always raised them up and embraced them, and they loved

him all the more. They began to wish Absalom were king instead of David.

He created a network of spies and supporters, and encamped with his men in Hebron. He sent messengers to all the tribes of Israel, telling them to rise up and make him their king.

David did not want to fight his son for the throne; he preferred to give it to him. He left Jerusalem and went into exile. But it was not as simple as that. Not everyone wanted a new king, and thousands of men went along with David. The priests came, too, carrying the Ark of God with them as a sign that David was still their spiritual leader. "Take the Ark back to Jerusalem," David said to them. "If it is God's will I too will return there one day." He climbed the hills outside the city, bare-headed and bare-footed, weeping bitterly because the son whom he loved so dearly had turned away from him.

Absalom would not rest until he had the whole country under him. He declared war on his father. So David mustered his army together on the banks of the Jordan. He put Joab in command, telling him: "Whatever happens, deal gently with my son."

The two armies met in the forest of Ephron, and the battle between them lasted all day. By nightfall, most of Absalom's men lay dead and Absalom himself had fled.

As he galloped through the woods on his mule, with David's men close behind, Absalom's long hair caught in the boughs of a tree. He was swept out of his saddle and hung there, dangling, until his enemies came up. They sent for Joab, who killed him.

When David heard of Absalom's death he climbed into a tower above the city gate and cried:

"Oh, Absalom, my son, I wish I had died instead of you! Oh, Absalom, my son!"

The Judgment of Solomon

OLOMON was still a young man when his father died and he became king.

One night God asked him in a dream, "What do you want from me, Solomon?"

The king replied, "Give me wisdom, God, and a knowledge of good and evil."

God was pleased, and promised Solomon all he had asked for and more besides.

Solomon did not have to wait long to put his new gifts to use. On his return to Jerusalem he found two women waiting at the palace for him.

Solomon seated himself on the throne and the women were brought before him. Each carried in her arms a baby wrapped in a cloth. One was kicking and crying; the other lay quite still. It was dead. The dead and the living children were laid at the king's feet.

"My lord," one of the women began, "I am the mother of the living child—"

"It's mine," the other woman cut in. "It was born to me on the same night that this woman had her baby. She lay on her child, and it died."

"No, my lord, that woman is lying. It was she who slept after her child was born, and she who smothered it by lying on it, so that it died. My child is alive. It is here, in front of you. Say that it is mine!" she begged.

King Solomon looked first at one woman and then at the other. Then he looked down at the baby kicking at his feet.

"Which of you is telling the truth?" he asked.

"I am, my lord," one of them said. "While I slept this woman came and stole my child and put her dead one in its place."

"You are lying!" the other woman exclaimed.

The baby began to cry. Solomon looked down at it again, and then back to the women.

"One child cannot belong to two mothers," he said. "One of you is lying to me. Which one is it?"

"Not I, my lord," insisted one woman.

"Not I," cried the other.

King Solomon turned to one of the guards standing behind his throne.

"Bring me a sword," he commanded.

Then he turned to the people who were gathered in the court and addressed them.

"God has called these two women before us," he said, "and they have brought me this child. Each wants me to tell her she is the real mother. Since both want the child, they must each have one half of it!"

With that the young king signalled to the soldier with the sword.

"This child shall be cut in two and divided equally between you," he said.

There was a terrible silence. Just as the sword was about to come down over the child the real mother ran forward. She caught the soldier by the arm, crying out:

"No! Don't kill him! Let her have my son!"

King Solomon turned to her. The soldier lowered his sword.

"Keep your son," the king said gently. He picked the baby up and put it into her arms.

The Visit of the Queen of Sheba

As God had foretold, Solomon's fame spread throughout the world. People came to hear his words of wisdom, and stayed to admire his palaces. He had created a world of unbelievable splendour around him. Gardens with fountains playing in them, stables filled with swift horses, chariots made of gold, a Temple that was like a great, bright jewel—all these dazzled the whole world with their magnificence.

Merchants came to Solomon's court with their pack animals laden with rare and precious goods from distant countries, and took news of its splendour back with them. His own camel trains crossed deserts and his great ships ploughed across the seas, further than ever before. News of this kingdom reached Sheba, where a wise queen ruled. She decided to see Solomon and his country for herself.

Because she was a queen, and as proud and mighty as any monarch on earth, she brought with her splendid presents for the king. Her camels and her slaves carried herbs

to heal and spices to eat, oils to anoint the body and perfume to sweeten it. She brought gifts of gold and silks and precious stones.

The arrival of the queen of Sheba was as splendid as anything that King Solomon's city had ever seen. Solomon, dressed in magnificent robes heavy with gold, awaited her, sitting on his throne. The queen came in, clothed in silks and pearls, rubies and damask, with a retinue of slaves carrying her gifts. She stood in front of him.

Then the queen tested Solomon's wisdom. As was customary in those days, she set him riddles. She questioned him about everything under the sun, and on every point the king answered her. His words were as bright and clear as his own jewels.

Then the king led her to a banquet in his palace. The food he served was cooked with spices and herbs as rare as those the queen of Sheba had brought him, and rich perfumes scented the air. When they had eaten together the queen said to Solomon:

"All the things that people say about you are true, though I did not believe them until I came and saw you with my own eyes. But the stories do not tell even half of what is here; your wisdom and your splendour are greater than any praise that has been given them. Let me stay a while longer, my lord, to see all the riches that your God has given you."

Then Solomon showed her everything in the land: the ministries that governed the people, the temples and their priests, the courts of justice. He showed her the great ships at anchor, the mines and the furnaces where the smiths smelted metal. He showed her, above all, the place where thinkers from all nations came together to talk and listen – to listen to Solomon as he spoke with the wisdom and understanding that God had given him.

Then the queen blessed the God of Solomon and the land of Israel, and went home.

67

The Parting of Elijah and Elisha

AFTER the death of Solomon, Israel was divided into two kingdoms. The prophet Elijah was sent to turn the people back from their evil ways.

After many years Elijah met a young man ploughing, called Elisha, whom God said was to succeed him. Elijah threw his cloak Elisha as a symbol that he was calling him to be his pupil. At once Elisha stopped ploughing, went to say goodbye to his family, and joined Elijah in his work.

The old prophet and the new had been together about seven years when Elijah said to Elisha:

"I must leave you and go on a journey."

"I will come with you," said Elisha, and they set out together for Bethel. Both prophets knew that this would be Elijah's last journey, his journey to God. So they walked towards Bethel, preaching to the people about the only true God, and teaching them to renounce all others.

When they reached the town, Elijah said:

"Stay here, Elisha. I must go on to Jericho."

Elisha knew that his teacher's time on earth was short. "I will come with you," he insisted.

At Jericho they were met by a group of other prophets.

"Do you know that God will take your master away from us today?" they asked Elisha.

"I know," Elisha replied. "Don't say any more."

The old prophet turned to Elisha. "Stay here," he said. "God is calling me. I must go to the river Jordan as he commands."

"I will come with you," Elisha replied.

So they left Jericho, and 50 of the prophets went with them. When they reached the banks of the river the prophets saw Elijah take off his cloak and roll it up. They saw him strike the river with it. The river divided and the two men crossed over the dry river bed and disappeared from the prophets' view.

As they crossed, Elijah said:

"What can I do for you before I go?"

"Give me your spirit," Elisha replied. "Give me a double portion of it, like the inheritance a father gives to his eldest son."

Elijah understood. "I shall soon be taken from you by a miracle," he said. "If you see this take place, you will know that God has given you my spirit. If not, then God has not chosen you."

Suddenly the sky opened and a chariot drawn by horses of fire came down to them. A whirlwind arose. It came between Elijah and Elisha and lifted Elijah into the chariot, and the chariot into the sky.

"My father, my father!" Elisha cried. "The horses and the chariots of Israel!"

He picked up the cloak that Elijah had dropped, and put it over his shoulders. The spirit of Elijah was in him.

He went back to the Jordan and struck the river water with Elijah's cloak. The water divided before him, and he walked over the dry bed to join the prophets who were waiting for him on the other side.

Shadrach, Meshach and Abed-nego

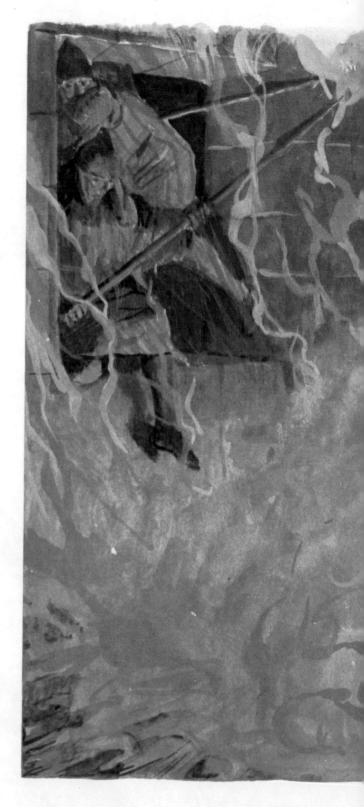

THE northern kingdom of Israel had been destroyed by the Assyrians, and later the southern kingdom of Judah came under the power of Babylon. King Nebuchadnezzar destroyed Jerusalem and exiled the Jews to Babylon. Then he built a huge gold statue, commanding that any man who did not worship it was to be thrown into a fiery furnace and burned to death.

Then the king was told that three Jews, Shadrach, Meshach and Abed-nego, who had been chosen by him to be brought up in the royal household, had refused to worship the idol.

"Let them die!" exclaimed the king. "Throw them into the furnace!"

The king ordered the fires in the furnace to be stoked hotter than ever before. The king's guards bound Shadrach, Meshach and Abed-nego. Then they led them up to the furnace and threw them inside. The heat was so great that the guards themselves were burned to death by the flames.

The fire leaped up over the three young men as they raised their arms to heaven. The flames licked their bodies and roared around them. Shadrach, Meshach and Abed-nego stood in the middle of the furnace, wrapped around by flames, but they remained completely unharmed and quite calm.

Nebuchadnezzar watched the spectacle with amazement. He called to his counsellors:

"Did we not throw three men, bound with ropes, into the fire?"

"We did, my lord," they replied.

"But I can see four men, unbound, walking in it! I can see them clearly—and the

fourth man looks like an angel or a god!"

Nebuchadnezzar walked up to the furnace and called through the flames:

"Come out, you servants of God!"

Shadrach, Meshach and Abed-nego walked out through the furnace's closed gates. The ropes that had bound them were gone. A great crowd of people gathered around them to see what sort of men these were, who could survive being thrown into the flames. Not a hair on their heads was singed, and there was not even the smell of smoke on their clothes.

Nebuchadnezzar raised his arms.

"Blessed be the God of Shadrach, Meshach and Abed-nego!" he cried.

The Writing on the Wall

WHEN Nebuchadnezzar died his son, Belshazzar, reigned in his place. One day the new king gave a feast for all the princes and nobles of his kingdom. He called for wine and then for more; soon, he began to grow drunk.

"Fetch me the drinking cups of the Jews," he called to his servants. "The ones my father Nebuchadnezzar took from the altars of their Temple. We will drink from them tonight."

So the holy vessels stolen from the Temple of God in Jerusalem were brought in, and filled with wine. The goblets and bowls were handed to Belshazzar's courtiers and his concubines, and they drank from them. The king held up his goblet of hammered gold.

"Let us praise the god of gold!" he called. The men and women around him took up the cry. They praised the gods of silver, of bronze and of iron, and drank to them out of the sacred cups. Then they praised the gods of wood and of stone, and drank yet again.

Suddenly the words the king was about to speak died away on his lips. On the wall opposite him there appeared a hand. Its fingers began to move, and it wrote four words. Then it faded away, but the writing did not. The king's face paled and his body shook with fear.

"What does it mean?" he asked. But no one could tell him. He called loudly for his magicians and wise men.

"Whoever can read this writing and interpret it for me," he said, "will be rewarded with riches and honour."

The wise men looked for a long time at the writing on the wall, but they could neither read it nor interpret it. Then the queen came into the hall.

"Why do you look so pale, my lord?" she asked. "I know of a man who can tell you the meaning of the words. His name is Daniel and he is a Jew. He has often in the past read omens for your father."

Belshazzar sent for Daniel. He pointed to the writing on the wall.

"Tell me what it means," he said, "and I will reward you with gold and honour."

"Keep your gold and your honour, my lord," Daniel replied. "The hand you saw was the hand of God. In your pride you drank out of the holiest vessels of God's Temple, and you defiled them. You have praised the gods of silver and of gold, but you have not spoken of the glory of the one God who has all men in his keeping. The writing on the wall is this: *mene mene tekel u-pharsin*. It means that the days of your kingdom are numbered, and that it will soon fall. It means that God has judged your actions and found them unworthy of you. It means that your enemies the Medes and the Persians will divide your kingdom between them."

Daniel spoke the truth. Before the night was over the king of the Medes attacked Babylon, killed Belshazzar and made his lost kingdom into part of the Median Empire.

Daniel in the Lions' Den

DANIEL knew more and was wiser than any man in Babylon. Darius the Great, the king of the Medes and the Persians, sent for him and said:

"I am going to put new governors in my provinces—there will be 120 of them. They will answer to three presidents. I want you to be their chief. There will be no one in the land more powerful than you, except myself."

To Darius it did not matter that Daniel was not a Babylonian but a Jew—a stranger in the land. But it did matter to the princes, governors and presidents who all had to answer to Daniel. They were jealous because he had more power than they, and they began to hate him. So they started to look about them for a way of removing him from the king's favour, of destroying him completely.

But Daniel was an honourable man and did his work well; it was difficult to find anything that could be held against him. He was the king's favourite, and rarely left his master.

"He never seems to break the law," his enemies said, "and he does everything the king commands. But he is a Jew, and his obedience to his God is even greater than his obedience to the king. We will set a trap for him that will lead to his death."

The princes, presidents and governors went to Darius. They bowed low to him, and then they said:

"King Darius, live for ever! May your power over the people never grow less. We have drawn up a law to test the good will and loyalty of your people here in Babylon. You must forbid everyone to pray to any god or ask a favour of any power but your

own. If a man wants something, he must ask the king and the king alone."

"Why do you want to make this law?" the king said to them.

"Because there are some people in Babylon who are in touch with your enemies and they may betray you," his advisers replied.

"I think it would be sufficient to make

this law last only for the next 30 days,"
Darius suggested. "That should give us
time to find out if any man is not loyal to
us."

This did not worry the princes because
they knew they could trap Daniel with the
law in less than a day. "How will you
punish anyone who disobeys the law?" one
of them asked the king.

"What would you suggest?" Darius asked.

"We say that any man who breaks this law
—which is a law of the Medes and Persians
and therefore can never be changed—should
die by being thrown to the lions," the prince

answered. Like other rich men, the king kept lions in a pit in his gardens, so that he could set them free when he wanted to, and hunt them for sport.

So Darius, who believed in the good faith of his advisers, signed the order, and his words became law.

When Daniel heard about the king's new law he was deeply distressed, because he knew he would have to break it, even if it cost him his life. He went home to his house and slowly climbed the flight of stairs outside it to the room on the top of the flat roof where he prayed to God. Every Jewish house had a room set aside where men went three times each day to pray.

Daniel opened the windows and looked westwards, towards Jerusalem. He remembered that he was an exile in a foreign land, that his people had been banished from their country because they had angered God.

"Forgive us, Lord," he prayed. "Make us better people. Help us to understand you."

Daniel's enemies had gathered around the house. They knew where the room was in which he said his prayers to God, and when they saw him at the window, they knew they had enough evidence to trap him.

They hurried to the king. "Didn't you sign an order, my lord, saying that any man who prayed to anyone other than yourself in the next 30 days would be thrown to the lions?" they asked.

"I did," said the king.

"We have found a man who has broken the order; he has disobeyed the king's command. He must die."

"He must," the king agreed. "What is his name?"

"His name is Daniel, and he is one of the Jews."

Darius was dismayed. Daniel was his most trusted servant; he knew that he was more loyal than all the princes in the land. He looked for a way to save him, but could find

76

none In the evening Daniel's enemies returned to the palace.

"Remember," they warned, "that the king's word is law. It is the law of the Medes and Persians, which may never be changed."

It seemed to Darius that he had no choice. Sadly, he ordered Daniel to be arrested. When his friend and adviser was brought to him in chains, he tried to bring him hope.

"You serve your God so faithfully, Daniel," he said. "Surely he will save you."

Daniel was led to the side of the pit. The lions were prowling about below, roaring because they were hungry. The king's guards threw Daniel into the pit and rolled a stone over the top to cover it. The king himself sealed the stone with the royal seal, so that no one could break in and rescue Daniel. Then he went back to the palace and prayed all night for his friend.

At sunrise he returned to the pit, broke the seals and rolled back the stone. He was trembling.

"Are you there, Daniel?" he called out.

"Yes, my lord. My God has saved me. I am alive and well. The lions are sleeping around me."

The king was overjoyed. "Oh, Daniel, my friend," he cried. "Praised be your God!"

Then he gave orders that all his people should gather to see the miracle. Daniel was lifted out of the pit and brought to the king. There was not a scratch on him. The lions had not touched Daniel because he had put his trust in God. But when the wicked advisers were thrown into the pit to punish them, the lions leaped on them at once and tore them to pieces, and ate them.

So Darius issued a new decree. It read:

"Throughout my lands men must worship the God of Daniel, for he is the only true God. His power will never end. He is a saviour and a worker of wonders in heaven and on earth, because he has brought his servant Daniel safely out of the lions' den."

God's Testing of Job

A GOOD man once lived in the land of Uz, and his name was Job. He loved God and used to pray to him every day before he went out to work on his farm. He was helped in everything he did by his sons and daughters, and was loved and respected by all.

"It's all very well to be good like Job when everything is going well," scoffed Satan, the Devil, to God, "but he'd soon lose courage if things went wrong with him. Let's say if he lost all his children, or his farm, or if he fell really ill – he wouldn't love you then!"

So God decided to test Job.

He let all these things happen to him, and, just as Satan had predicted, Job grew bitter and angry. His friends tried to tell him why God allows us to feel pain – to make us see things more clearly, to make us less proud, to make us into stronger people.

Then God himself spoke to Job. He reminded him that men know so little about life, let alone about anything that goes on beyond it. Job was impatient.

"But why, why, *why*, Lord?" he asked.

Then God stopped talking and appeared before him. Now Job no longer needed the answers. He was filled with peace, and with the fullness and glory of God's presence.

Jonah and the Whale

JONAH was going about his daily work when God spoke to him.

"Jonah," he said. "I want you to go to Nineveh. The people there are wicked. Tell them that their city and everything in it will be destroyed within 40 days."

"Why choose me, Lord?" Jonah replied in dismay. "Why should I, an ordinary Jew in Israel, go to preach about God to people I don't know, who live far away, and who are not even Jews and don't believe in you? Besides, you are a kind and merciful God; you would never wipe out a whole city like that."

He decided not to go. But he was afraid of God's anger, and tried to escape by going on board a ship bound for Tarshish, in the opposite direction to Nineveh. The ship set sail and Jonah fell asleep in the hold.

Suddenly a great storm blew up and the captain shook Jonah awake.

"Come," he said. "Perhaps it's your God who is angry with us." Jonah prayed, but the storm grew worse. "Look," he said to the sailors, "I know it's my fault; you had better throw me overboard."

The sailors did not want to do that, so they rowed hard, trying to get back to land.

But the hurricane blew more fiercely than ever, so they dropped Jonah overboard.

The winds died down at once. At first Jonah floated on the waves, but not for long. A great fish, like a whale, came and swallowed him up, and for three days and three nights he lay inside its belly. Then the fish spat him out, safe, onto the beach.

Again God commanded Jonah to go to Nineveh, and this time he obeyed at once. He arrived at the great city and walked through the streets, calling out, "In 40 days Nineveh will be destroyed!"

The people who heard him were afraid, for they believed in God's power. They took Jonah to the king, and the king ordered that every man and woman in the city should pray for forgiveness for their wickedness and resolve to begin a new life. God was pleased with their prayers and spared Nineveh.

Jonah, however, was angry with God. He felt that he had been made to look a fool. "I knew all along that you wouldn't kill them," he grumbled.

He went out into the desert and sat down. The sun grew hot and uncomfortable, so God made a tree grow over him to give him shade. The next day the tree withered and died and the sun scorched Jonah until he began to feel very ill.

"I'm sorry for that tree; it lived such a short time," said Jonah to himself. "I wish I were dead too."

Then God spoke gently to him. "If you feel sorry for this tree, which you neither planted nor watered, how much more sorry I would have been, to have had to destroy Nineveh. My love is greater than yours. I forgive those who repent, and I bring comfort to all men."

The New Testament

CONTENTS

An Angel Visits Mary

CENTURIES passed. The land of Judah became part of the Roman Empire, but it remained a separate kingdom, called Judaea, ruled by Herod, a Jewish king.

God sent the angel Gabriel to the town of Nazareth in Galilee, to visit a young girl. She had been promised in marriage to a man named Joseph, who was descended from the family of David. The girl's name was Mary.

The angel appeared to her and said, "Greetings, Mary, God's blessing is on you." When Mary saw the angel and heard what he said she was filled with wonder and unease.

"Do not be afraid, Mary," the angel continued, "God loves you; he has filled you with his grace. You will have a child, a son whom you will call Jesus. He will be great, and people will call him the Son of the Highest. God will give him the throne of his forefather David, and he will reign over Israel for ever. His kingdom will never cease to exist."

"How can this be?" asked Mary. "I have never slept with a man."

The angel Gabriel replied, "The Holy Spirit of God is with you; God will take possession of you. And because of this, the holy child that will be born from your body will be called the Son of God."

The angel went on, "Through God's will your cousin Elizabeth will also have a son. You know she could not have children before and seemed too old to bear any now, but she will give birth before you. God can make everything possible."

Mary said, "I am God's servant. May everything happen just as you have said."

The Birth of Jesus

THE months passed from spring to summer, and then to autumn. The child that Mary carried slept in her and grew. Winter came, and Mary's body was heavy and full. It was time for her child to be born.

Now that Judaea was part of the Roman Empire Mary and Joseph had to obey the laws of Rome. "Every man and woman who lives in our lands must pay tax," went the proclamation of the Emperor Augustus. "A new register will be drawn up, on which the name of every citizen is written. The Emperor wants a complete record of his people."

When King Herod heard this command, he ordered everyone in his kingdom to return to the place of their birth to be put on the register. Because Joseph belonged to the family of David, he had to leave Nazareth where he lived and worked, and go back to Bethlehem, which lay some 70 miles to the south.

As his wife, Mary had to go too, although her child was expected any day. Together they set off on their mule over the hills to Bethlehem. In the evening they arrived in the city, and tried to find somewhere to stay. But Joseph was poor and the streets were crowded with people.

"Go away," the people said. "Bethlehem is full of outsiders like you, coming in from the hills and valleys to be registered." They looked at Mary, who sat tired and heavy on the mule. "Move off," they said, and sent her away.

Night had fallen, and Joseph wrapped his cloak around Mary and led her down the street. He knocked at the door of another house. A woman opened it a crack to look at them. "No room," she said firmly, and shut the door in their faces.

Now Mary slipped gently off the mule, because it too was tired. They walked on until they came to an inn. Lamps burned in every window and the rooms inside were full of people eating and drinking. Horses, camels and donkeys stood munching their hay in the courtyard. Joseph knocked on the door. The landlord opened it.

"No room at the inn!" he called out, and waved them away. As they moved on, the light from the door fell on Mary.

"You can sleep in the stable, if you like. The straw there is fresh," the landlord called after her.

So Mary made a bed for herself in the sweet-smelling hay. And there, with the ox and the donkey beside her, she gave birth to her son. She wrapped him up well and laid him in a manger filled with hay. She called him Jesus, which means, "God Saves".

That night the words of the prophet Isaiah came true:

"For unto us a child is born; unto us a son is given;
And the government shall be upon his shoulders,
And his name shall be
Wonderful, Counsellor, the Prince of Peace,
The Mighty God, The Everlasting Father."

In the hills around Bethlehem shepherds were out in the fields, taking care of their flocks during the night. Suddenly an angel appeared to them, and the glory of God shone around them. The shepherds were terrified because there was so much light.

"Don't be afraid," the angel said to them. "I have good news for you – tonight a Saviour has been born to you in Bethlehem, the city of David. His name is Christ, the Lord."

Then the light increased so that its splendour lit up the fields as if it was day, and the sky was filled with the angels of God. Their voices rose like the wind and swept over the hills and valleys as they sang:

"Glory to God in the highest, and on earth peace, good will towards men!"

Then the light and the music gradually faded away and the shepherds said to one another:

"Come, let's go to Bethlehem and see the holy thing that has happened there!"

They ran down into the town and came to the stable where Mary and Joseph were resting. They saw the baby sleeping in the manger, and kneeled down and worshipped it.

Then they went out and told the people of Bethlehem what had happened, and everyone was astonished.

Mary treasured all these memories and thought about them often as Jesus grew up.

The Visit of the Wise Men

THE people of Judaea did not realize that a star had risen over Bethlehem. They did not notice that the nights were no longer dark, that a new star, brighter than any other had appeared in the sky, directly above the stable where Jesus had been born.

King Herod himself first heard of the star through strangers when three wise men came to visit him from the East.

"What is this light that has appeared over your country?" they asked. "We have noticed a new star in heaven. It does not move like the other stars, but stays fixed in place above one spot in Judaea."

Herod looked at the wise men. They were old, and obviously skilled at understanding and interpreting the movements of stars and their meanings. But he could not understand what they were talking about. Their next question took him quite by surprise.

"Where is this child who is born to be king of the Jews?" they asked.

"Born to be *what*?" he exclaimed.

"King of the Jews. We think he is the Messiah, the Saviour that all the world is waiting for. That is why we are here."

Herod did not like the idea at all. *He* was king of the Jews and he wanted no one to take his place. He called for his high priests and scholars.

"What do you know about a new king of Judaea?" he asked. "Is it true that we are to have a Messiah?"

"Yes, my lord, it is true. The writings of the prophets say so," the priests replied.

"When? Where?" the king demanded.

One of the scholars came forward. "It's all written down in the book of the prophet Micah, sir," he said. "It's to happen in Bethlehem. This is how Micah puts it—the language is old-fashioned but the meaning is clear—'*And thou Bethlehem, in the land of Judah, art not the least among the princes of Judah: for out of thee shall come a Government that shall rule my people Israel.*'"

Herod had heard enough. He turned to the strangers. "Find this king," he said. "And come back and tell me where he is.

I want to go and – er – worship him too."

The wise men set out and once again the star stood out, brilliantly clear, in the eastern sky. Its light drew them onwards, and they followed it until over Bethlehem it seemed to stand still.

There they found Mary and Joseph, and the baby Jesus, lying in the hay. They knew this was the king they had come so far to find, and they fell down on their knees and worshipped him.

Then each man reached into his saddle bags and drew out the present he had brought. Gently they laid their gifts in the hay around the child.

They gave gold, which was a gift for kings, and frankincense, which was burned on the altar of God. And they gave myrrh, which was used in those days to help preserve men's bodies after death.

The Flight into Egypt

"Do not tell King Herod where to find Jesus," God said to the wise men in a dream, "And do not go back the way you came. Leave Israel secretly."

The wise men obeyed promptly; by the time Herod's spies realized what had happened, they were far away.

Then Joseph, too, received a message from God. An angel appeared to him in a dream and said:

"Joseph, you are in great danger. Herod wants to kill the child. He is looking for you everywhere. Take Mary and the baby and flee with them to Egypt. Stay there until I tell you to return. Hurry!"

Joseph woke up. Everything seemed quiet around him. Then somewhere a dog barked. He rose quickly and slipped on his sandals. Then he shook Mary gently.

"Wake up, Mary!" he said. "We must escape before King Herod finds us!"

"May God be with us," said Mary, and wrapped Jesus in her cloak.

They left Bethlehem as they had come,

riding on a mule. But this time Mary carried the child in her arms, and the night seemed to fold itself around them and hide them from men's eyes. By sunrise they were far away to the south, and when they had crossed the border into Egypt they knew they were safe.

Herod, meanwhile, was waiting impatiently for the wise men to return. As the days and weeks passed, his impatience changed to suspicion. At last he sent his spies to hunt for them.

"Why, they've been gone a long time, now!" the people in Bethlehem said. "They went somewhere in that direction," and they waved towards the eastern hills.

When Herod heard how he had been tricked he fell into a fury. He tried to remember exactly what it was that the wise men had said. They had mentioned a child king, and they had gone to Bethlehem.

He was determined to resist any claim to his throne, but he had no idea where to find the child that the wise men had said would be king. He did not even know its name. He only knew that it lived in Bethlehem and could not be more than two years old. In a fit of jealous fear he commanded that all children in Bethlehem under two years of age should be killed.

His soldiers marched into the town, snatched the terrified children from their mothers' arms and killed every one of them. A terrible wailing filled the air, as the mothers of Bethlehem sat down in the streets with their dead babies in their arms, mourning and weeping for the children they had lost.

Time passed. Another king sat on the throne of Judaea. Mary and Joseph were still living in Egypt, and Jesus had grown into a young boy. Then an angel came to Joseph in a dream and said, "Go back to Israel, for Herod the King is dead." So they returned to Israel, and settled in Nazareth.

John the Baptist Baptizes Jesus

FOR hundreds of years the Jews had been waiting for their Saviour to come. They were longing for someone to free them from Roman rule and from the hateful taxes they had to pay.

John was first to recognize that Jesus was the Saviour everyone was waiting for. He was Jesus' cousin, six months older than he, and as a priest's son he had been brought up to serve in the Temple in Jerusalem. He saw there how the rich ill-treated the poor, and he soon came to feel that God was not present in the Temple with its greedy, weak priests.

So John went into the desert, wearing a rough shirt of camel's hair, a leather belt round his waist, and his hair hanging to his shoulders. He ate locusts and wild honey, and drank water from a goat skin he filled at desert wells. He lived in caves, waiting for God to speak to him.

One day he felt a great stillness lying over the hills. Then God said to him:

"Call the people of Israel; prepare them for the coming of their Lord."

John did not go to the towns; he began preaching where he was, in the desert. People came because they were curious, and stayed because they believed.

"Prepare!" he cried, "Prepare for the Kingdom of God! Stop offering sacrifices in the Temple; stop doing wrong to your neighbours!"

He baptized the people by dipping their bodies in the river Jordan, as a sign that everything wrong in them was washed away and they intended to try to live better lives in future and follow God's commandments.

"What do we do now?" the people asked.

"If you have two coats, give one to the man who has none," he replied. "If you have enough food, give half of it to those who are hungry."

Some tax collectors who had come to be baptized asked him, "What shall we do?"

"Be honest," he said. "Don't take money from others and keep it for yourselves."

Then some soldiers said to him, "And what about us?"

"Don't hurt other people," John replied, "and be content with your pay."

"Who are you, anyway?" they asked. "Are you Elijah? Or the prophet we await?"

John answered, "I am just a voice crying out in the desert. Prepare the way for the Lord! I am not the Saviour, the Christ. He will follow me and will be much more powerful than I. I baptize you with water, but he will baptize you with God's spirit and with fire. I am not worthy to touch even his shoes!"

When Jesus heard about John he left Nazareth and went to look for him. He found him on the banks of the Jordan and asked John to baptize him.

"That isn't right," John said to him. "It is I who should be baptized by you, for you are greater than I!"

Jesus answered, "It is God's will."

So John baptized Jesus in the river. As he was coming out of the water the skies seemed to open and he saw the spirit of God coming towards him in the shape of a dove. The voice of God said:

"You are my beloved Son, and I am very pleased with you."

The Temptation in the Wilderness

GOD sent Jesus into the wilderness. He went alone into a desert far from the river Jordan where everything was dry and nothing grew.

There was silence around him. Elijah had once come here, and had wandered for 40 days and 40 nights over the stones and sand. Moses, before him, had counted 40 days go by as he spoke to God on Mount Horeb. Now it was Christ who stood in the waste land, and over whom 40 days and 40 nights were to pass.

He was hungry. Wherever he looked there was sand and there was stone. Even the wood that had once grown here had turned to stone.

He grew hungrier and he longed for bread. The wind blew waves of hot sand along the ground and threw it into his face.

"If you are the Son of God," the voice of the Devil said through the wind, "you can do anything you like. You can begin by turning these stones into bread!"

But Jesus replied, "Man does not live on bread alone; he needs the word of God."

Night fell, and the Devil carried Jesus to the holy city of Jerusalem. Here, from the highest ledge of the Temple, Jesus could see the domes and spires and the pools of water lying in their beauty below him.

"If you are the Son of God," the Devil whispered through the night wind, "you can throw yourself down into the city. The angels of God will hold you and will not let you fall. The time has come; show the people that you are God. They will believe you and will make you king."

"No," said Jesus. "It is not for me to test God. He has sent me to share the pain and suffering of men."

The Devil took Jesus still higher. He took him to the highest mountain in the world. From here Jesus could see everything on earth from the beginning to the end of time. He saw the great kingdoms, the armies and the weapons of all mankind.

The Devil tempted him for the third time. "I can give you all these things," he said, "I will make you more powerful than any man has ever been. All you have to do is bow to me and worship me!"

Jesus cried out, "Go away, Satan–I cannot worship you; I cannot worship any-

thing but God. The Commandments tell us,
'*You shall worship God, and God alone*'!"

Then the Devil went away, and with him
went all the evil and darkness that had filled
the air. The angels of God came and brought
Jesus food and took care of him.

The Marriage at Cana

A MAN and a girl were getting married in Galilee. The wedding was being held in the village of Cana, and Jesus was one of the guests.

The feast had already gone on for several days. This was the last evening of the wedding, when the bride would be led to the bridegroom's house. She would be taken there at night, by torchlight, and she would be hidden from curious eyes by her long veil, with garlands of myrtle and orange blossom in her hair, and wound around her waist.

Jesus had brought his new disciples to the wedding with him. Mary his mother was there too; her husband Joseph had died many years before.

The family had invited everyone in the village to join in the feasting. A crowd of people filled the house and sat outside under the trees, eating and drinking and enjoying themselves.

Mary came up to Jesus quietly and waited until she could speak to him without being overheard.

"They have run out of wine," she said. "More people came to the wedding than were expected. The old wine's all gone and the new wine's turned sour."

"Can't they send out for more?" asked Jesus.

"No. You know how poor they are. All the money's gone on this food and the wine. They feel so ashamed."

"Why do you tell me all this?" asked Jesus. "The time when I can help has not come yet."

Jesus spoke these words gently. Mary still believed that he would help his friends.

"Do whatever he tells you to," she said to the servants.

They went back into the house. The wineskins had run dry, but the guests did not know this yet. They were watching the drummer and the flute player, whose beat and shrill piping filled the air. The rhythm was getting faster; the people clapped in time to it while their feet pounded into the hard earth on the floor.

In the corner stood six large stone water jars, where it was customary for people to

wash their hands and feet as they entered the house. The spouts of the jars were stuffed with fresh green leaves, to keep the water cool. Jesus called to a servant:

"Fill these jars to the brim."

The servant drew the water from the well in the yard, and filled the jars.

"Now pour some off into smaller pitchers and take it to the chief guest," he said.

They carried the pitchers to the man and he drank from them, tasting each one in turn. He paused, then he laughed.

"Why, what wine is this?" he exclaimed, "I've never tasted anything like it!" He called across to the bridegroom:

"Other people serve their good wine first, and keep the poorer stuff to the end. But you have kept this wine, the best I've ever tasted, till now!"

The people were amazed. Everyone knew that the jars had been filled with water from the well. They looked at Jesus. Through the power God had given him he had turned water into wine. It was his first miracle.

The Choosing of the Twelve Apostles

Jesus was walking by the Sea of Galilee early one morning when he saw two fishermen in the distance, cleaning their nets. When he came closer he saw they were Simon and Andrew, his first two disciples, who still carried on their trade as fishermen whenever they could. He looked down at their empty baskets.

"Simon," he said, "Row over there, where the water is deep. That is where you will find the fish!"

"Oh, Master," Simon replied, "We've

had our nets out the whole night, and we've caught nothing. Still, if you think it's worth it, we will try over there."

He pushed his boat into the lake and his brother Andrew rowed out after him in the other. They hung the net between the boats, where the water lay deep. They waited, and a stillness spread over the lake. Suddenly Simon shouted for joy. From the shore Jesus could see the two men hauling in the net, weighed down with fish that jumped and flickered in the dawn light. They filled their boats with fish and rowed back. Simon was so excited that he jumped into the water and waded ashore. He threw himself down at Jesus' feet, exclaiming, "Leave me, Lord; I am not worthy of you."

"Come with me," Jesus said to him. "From now on you will both be fishers of men."

Simon and Andrew had two friends, James and John, the sons of Zebedee, who were fishing farther down the lake. Jesus called to them too, and they left their boats and their father, and followed him.

Then Jesus went down to the harbour. He saw a tax collector named Matthew sitting at the door of his customs house. Matthew looked up and Jesus said, "Follow me!"

The people were horrified. A tax collector ought not to be a disciple of Jesus. Why, everyone knew that they were thieves and swindlers. People like the Pharisees prided themselves on never having anything to do with them. Jesus heard the people grumbling, and he said:

"I have not come to heal the healthy, but the sick. I have not come to save people who do well, but to show them how they can do better."

Then he went up into the hill country. He chose twelve men from among all his disciples, to be his apostles, and spread his teaching. They were Peter and his brother Andrew, James and John, the sons of Zebedee, Philip, Bartholomew, Thomas, Matthew, another man called James, the son of Alphaeus, Thaddaeus (who is sometimes known as Jude), Simon the Zealot, and Judas Iscariot.

Jesus sent his disciples out, two by two, in different directions. He laid his hands on them, to bless them and give them his power.

"Take nothing with you, not even money or a spare pair of sandals," he said. "When you enter a village, greet the people there and say 'Shalom', 'Peace be with you'. If they welcome you, speak to them. Heal their sick, eat their bread. If they don't want to hear you, leave them. Don't be afraid; God will be with you. He will tell you what to say. Remember the harvest is ripe; keep praying that others will come to help you reap it."

The Sermon on the Mount

Jesus went into the hills and said to the men and women who gathered around to listen to him:

"How blessed are people who can be humble, for the Kingdom of God will be theirs.

"How blessed are people who are sad, for they will find comfort.

"How blessed are those people who have no possessions, for they will possess the whole world.

"How blessed are those who long to see goodness triumph, for they will have their wish.

"How blessed are people who show mercy to their enemies, for they will receive mercy in their turn.

"How blessed are those whose hearts are pure, for they will see God.

"How blessed are the people who are peacemakers, for God will call them his children.

"How blessed are those who suffer for the cause they know to be good, for the Kingdom of God will be theirs.

"How blessed you are when men curse you and punish you because of your love for me. Accept their insults gladly, for your reward will be great later on."

"You are like salt, without which food has no taste. You are the light for the whole world, so don't hide your light away where no one can see it. When men see what good things you are doing, they will praise God, in whose service you are doing them.

"Don't save up treasure on earth, where moths and rust will eat it away and where thieves can break in and steal it; save up treasure for yourselves in heaven where it cannot spoil and will never be stolen. For your heart will always be where the things you value are.

"Don't judge other people or they will judge you. It is easy to see the speck of dust in your friend's eye, but not so easy to admit that you have a big splinter in your own.

"First, you must take out the splinter in your own eye, then perhaps you will be able to see clearly enough to remove the dust from someone else's.

"You have heard men say, 'An eye for an eye and a tooth for a tooth.' But I say to you, it is no good fighting evil with evil. If a man hits your face on one side, offer him the other side too.

"You have heard men say, 'Love your neighbour and hate your enemy.' But I say to you, love your enemy and pray for those who hate you. Always treat other people as you would like them to treat you.

"When you pray, speak to God simply, for he knows what you need even before you ask him.

"Ask and you will get what you ask for; look and you will find what you are looking for; knock and the door will be opened.

"Every man who hears my words and follows them is like the wise man who built his house on rock. The rain fell and the floods came; the winds blew but the house did not fall down because it was built on rock. But every man who hears my words and does not follow them is like the foolish man who built his house on sand. The rain fell and the floods came; the winds blew and the house fell down because it had no foundations to hold it steady."

Jesus Calms the Storm

Jesus went on preaching to the crowds who were still gathered around him on the mountain. He said:

"No man can serve two masters; either he will hate the one and love the other, or be loyal to one and betray the other. You cannot serve both God and Money.

"So I tell you not to worry about what you should eat or what you should drink, nor what kind of clothes you should wear. Life is more important than the food that you eat, and the body is more important than the clothes that cover it.

"Look up at the birds flying in the sky. They don't sow crops nor reap them nor stow them away in barns—and yet your heavenly Father feeds them. Surely you are worth more than they are!

"Is there one of you who can make himself any taller, however hard he concentrates on worrying about it?

"So why worry about clothes? Look at the lilies growing in the field. They don't do any work and yet I tell you that Solomon in all his glory was not as splendid as they are. Now if that is how God clothes the grass in

the field which is growing today and is
withered tomorrow, surely he will take even
more pains to clothe you. How little faith
you have in him!

"So, don't waste your time worrying
about your daily needs; leave that for men
who have no God to serve. God knows your
needs. Concentrate on winning and deserv-
ing his love, then everything else will follow.

"Don't worry about tomorrow, for tomorrow will take care of itself."

It had grown late and night was falling.
Jesus had been speaking for many hours.
When he stopped at last, the crowds still sat
there, waiting. He said to his disciples:

"We must cross to the other side of the
lake."

So they left all the people behind and set
sail across the water.

The sky grew black with clouds, and a
sudden squall whipped up the waves and
smashed them into the boat. The men were
terrified, expecting any moment now to be
spilled into the water.

"Where is Jesus?" a voice screamed into
the storm. "We shall all die!" The rain
lashed down as they scrambled about the
boat looking for him. They found him,
asleep in the stern. They pulled at his cloak
to wake him.

"Rabbi! Master! Don't you care that we
are drowning?" He opened his eyes and
stood up. "Why are you afraid?" he asked.
"Where is your faith?"

Then he called to the storm:

"Peace! Be still!"

The storm died away and the waves sank
back into calm. Gradually, the stars appeared
through the clouds until the night sky
stretched clear and still over the earth. A
sense of wonder filled all the men in the
boat.

"Who can he be?" they whispered to one
another. "Even the storm obeys him!"

Jesus Heals a Madman

ONE day Jesus met a madman. The man was well known in the district; he lived in graveyards and used to shout and scream all night because his mind was in such agony. People had tried to tie him down with chains, but the maniac always broke loose from them and ran off into the hills.

This man saw Jesus coming across the lake in a boat and he ran down to the shore to meet him. He cried:

"What do you want from me, Jesus, son of the most high God? For his sake, don't hurt me!"

Jesus asked him gently, "What is your name?"

"My name is Million, because we are so many," replied the evil spirits that had taken over the poor man's mind.

"Come out of him!" Jesus called to the spirits. "Go into those pigs grazing on the hill instead!"

The evil spirits obeyed him. They took possession of the pigs, so that they in turn went mad. Snorting wildly they stampeded over the edge of the hill and fell to their deaths in the lake below.

The swineherd ran away, terrified, and told the story to everyone he met. People hurried to see what was happening. There he was—the madman whose mind had been possessed by the evil spirits—sitting beside Jesus, properly dressed and perfectly sane.

The people were frightened of Jesus' power, and begged him to leave their district. So he went back to the other side of the lake.

Jairus's Daughter

As the boat drew in a man called Jairus came running down to the shore. "It's my little daughter," he sobbed. "She's very ill. She's only twelve, and she is dying. Please come and lay your hands on her so that she will live!"

Jesus went with him, followed, as always, by a crowd. A woman who had heard that Jesus could heal managed to push her way close to him. She had been ill for twelve years, and had visited many doctors; but instead of curing her they had made her worse.

"If I can only touch his clothes," she thought, "I shall be cured."

She pushed forward and brushed against his robe. At once her sickness had gone.

Jesus stopped. "Who touched me?" he asked. "I felt power flow from me."

"I did, Lord," the woman said, "Forgive me!"

"Your faith has healed you," replied Jesus. "Go in peace."

A man pushed his way up to Jairus. "It is too late!" he cried. "Your child is dead!"

"Oh, no," replied Jesus quietly. "She is not dead, she is asleep. Only believe, and she will be cured."

Then he went into the house and sent away the women who had come to weep and mourn for the child. He went into the room where the little girl lay on her bed.

"Get up, my child!" he said, and took her hand in his. She opened her eyes and stood up. Jesus smiled at her. Then he said, "Bring her some food," and left the house.

103

The Death of John the Baptist

JOHN the Baptist was in prison. For a long time now he had been saying things that outraged the king, Herod Antipas. No one likes to be told that he is weak and greedy, that he is no good at his job. But Herod was all these things. In his greed he had even married his brother's wife, Herodias, and taken her daughter Salome to live with them in the palace.

Herodias had been brought up in Rome and was used to luxury. Like the Romans, she liked to spend money – other people's money – on spectacular displays of dancing and acrobatics. One year she and Herod took the court to live for a time in a fort by the Dead Sea.

They had not been there long before John the Baptist demanded to speak to the king. The queen was against letting him in; she was afraid of this outspoken preacher. But Herod was curious; he had heard that John was rousing the people against him. He wanted to see this wild man from the desert for himself. "If he is dangerous," he reassured Herodias, "I will put him in prison."

John came before the king barefooted and wearing his rough camel-hair shirt.

"You are evil!" he cried. "You stole your brother's wife! You rule badly and you demand money from the poor. God's kingdom is near! God will punish you!"

The king had John arrested. He was put in prison and left there for months while Herod Antipas made up his mind what to do with him. He did not kill him for fear that John's followers would rouse the people to rebellion.

While John waited in the darkness of his prison he sent a message to Jesus. "Are you really the Messiah," he asked, "or should we expect another?"

"Tell John," Jesus replied, "that I have given sight to the blind and made the lame walk. The lepers are healed and the deaf can hear. The dead are brought back to life and the poor are hearing the good news about God. Happy is the man who does not lose his faith in me."

Then John, too, waited, with peace in his heart.

One day the king gave a party. Every high official, commander, and noble was invited. Soon everyone was drunk with wine and music.

"Where's Salome?" the king cried. "I want her to dance for us!" So she danced, and the king went wild with excitement.

"I'll give you anything you like!" he shouted, "Just ask for it!"

The girl ran off to find her mother.

"What shall I ask for?" she whispered. "Ask for the head of John the Baptist," replied the queen.

When the king heard Salome's request he was dismayed. But because he was a weak man he had to pretend to the world that he was extra strong.

"Off with his head!" he cried.

So John the Baptist died, and his head was brought to Salome on a platter.

The Feeding of the Five Thousand

JESUS said to his disciples, "Come, let us go to a quiet place to rest." He set off with them by boat, but the people did not want him to go, and a great crowd followed him along the shore.

They seemed to be so lost, like sheep without a shepherd, that Jesus was filled with pity for them. He steered his boat back to the shore and spoke to them about God, and healed everyone who was sick.

Evening came, and the disciples said, "This is a lonely place and it's getting late. Send the people away, Lord, while it's still light, so that they can find themselves something to eat."

He answered, "Let them have our food. How much do we need to fill them all?"

Philip answered, "We need at least 200 pieces of silver to buy enough bread to fill all these people. There must be close on 5,000 of them. And there's no bread to buy."

"How much food have we got?" Jesus asked. Andrew came up with a small boy. "This little fellow's got five barley loaves and two fish," he said. "He says we can have them if we like. But that won't be enough to feed 5,000 people!"

Jesus said, "Tell everyone to sit down. Arrange them in small groups to make it easier to pass the food around."

Then he took the five loaves and two fish and looked up to heaven. He gave God thanks for the food, and broke the bread into pieces. Then he divided the fish, and gave all the pieces to the disciples and the small boy to distribute.

Everyone of the 5,000 people ate and no one went hungry. When they had all had enough Jesus said:

"Collect the food that is left over, so that nothing is wasted."

They picked up the remaining food and filled twelve baskets with the scraps.

Jesus Visits the Home of Mary and Martha

ON HIS way to Jerusalem Jesus stopped in the village of Bethany at the home of two sisters, Martha and Mary.

"Jesus has come to see us!" Martha called to her sister. She felt very important. "Quick! Get to work! We must show him what we can do. We'll give him a better meal than he'd have anywhere else. We don't want anyone to say we are poor or mean!"

She was in such a hurry that she hardly found time to greet Jesus properly as he entered. Mary fell on her knees, saying:

"Welcome, Lord. You bring joy and peace to us!" She led him through to the courtyard and he sat down. Then she sat down beside him, and he began to speak of God and of our need to empty our hearts of all things except his love. As Mary looked into Jesus' face and listened to his voice, a great calm came over her.

"What he says is more important than anything else in the world," she thought. "I must stay here with him, not go to the kitchen. I must live for this moment, not for later, when he is gone. God has given me this moment to enjoy."

Martha came out of the kitchen. Her face was red from the heat and the hurry, and her hands were wet with the fish she had cleaned. She was angry with her sister.

"Lord, won't you tell Mary to help me with the cooking?" she asked Jesus. "There's so much to do!"

"Martha, Martha," Jesus replied. "You worry too much about small things. Do one thing at a time, and only the most important. Mary knows what that is."

The two sisters looked at him. Had he not said once that his words were more than food and wine?

Later, Jesus said to his disciples:

"The Son of Man has come to give his life so that others may be set free."

Jesus often called himself the Son of Man. It was what the prophet Daniel had called the Messiah, the Saviour who would come one day to lead the people back to the Kingdom of God. The Son of Man was the secret name for Christ.

"You must not be sad," Jesus went on. "You must hold fast to your faith in God and your faith in me. The place where my Father will lead you when everything is over is large, like a house with many rooms. I am going there now, to get a place ready for you. One day I will come back to lead you there.

"Now you know where I am going and the road I will take to get there."

"But, Master," said Thomas, "that's just it. We don't know where you are going. So how can we know the way there?"

"I am the way, I am the truth and I am life," Jesus replied. "All you need to do is to follow me."

Lazarus

ONE day Lazarus fell ill, Martha and Mary sent a message to Jesus: "Hurry and heal our brother!" But Jesus' followers were frightened.

"Don't go back to Bethany!" they begged. "Not long ago the people tried to stone you."

"I must," replied Jesus. "Lazarus has already fallen asleep and I must wake him."

When they reached Bethany Lazarus had already died and, as was usual in hot countries, they had buried his body at once.

Martha sobbed, "If only you had come sooner, Lord, you could have saved him!"

"Lazarus will rise again," Jesus replied.

"Yes, I know that," said Martha, "When the day of resurrection comes–"

"I am the resurrection and I am life," Jesus told her. "If a man believes in me he will never die. Do you realize that?"

"Yes, Lord, I do," said Martha, "I believe you are Christ, the Son of God."

"Take me to his grave," said Jesus.

The grave was in a cave, and they had to roll a stone away from the entrance to open it. The people murmured, "Why didn't he save his friend Lazarus?"

Jesus wept. He wept because they did not understand that with God there is no death.

"Lazarus, come out!" he cried.

Shuffling, because his hands and feet were still bound in the winding sheet of the dead, Lazarus came out. The crowd of people gasped in amazement; all Jesus said was:

"Unbind him and let him go home."

The Entry into Jerusalem

Jesus prepared himself for the last stage of his journey. When people saw him going towards Jerusalem they were amazed. Everyone knew his enemies there were plotting how to kill him. But Jesus was going to Jerusalem to attend the feast of the Passover, when every Jewish household would sacrifice a lamb to God. Men believed that they would be made pure again because an innocent creature had died for them.

"The Passover will soon begin," Jesus told his disciples, "and the Son of Man will be betrayed by his own people, into the hands of the chief priests and Pharisees. Then he will be handed over to men who do not believe in God. They will jeer at him and spit in his face. They will beat him and kill him. But after three days he will rise again."

As Jesus approached Jericho he healed a blind beggar, who followed Jesus, praising God. Then all the people flocked around shouting, "Jesus of Nazareth is coming! They say that he's the Messiah!" The word went round from street to street.

People crowded along the roadside to see him pass. Among them was a man called Zacchaeus, who wanted to see Jesus more than anything else in the world. He tried to elbow his way to the front of the crowd, but the people pushed him back. No one liked him because he was a tax collector and had Romans as his friends. He was a little man,

and he knew that he would never see Jesus from behind all those people. So he climbed up a tree to get a better view.

Jesus walked by. Hundreds of people thronged about him, touching him and being blessed by him. Suddenly he looked up and saw Zacchaeus in the tree.

"Come down, Zacchaeus," he called, "Tonight I am going to stay at your house."

The next day Jesus set out for Jerusalem. He took two of his disciples aside and said to them:

"Go into the village on the slopes of the Mount of Olives. You will find a donkey there, which no one has yet ridden. Untie it and bring it here."

They brought the donkey to him, and he mounted it. Then they climbed up along the stony road that led towards the city.

Wherever he went the people threw their cloaks down in front of him on the dusty stones, as if they were laying a carpet for a king. Children plucked leaves off the hedges and scattered them before him, and strewed flowers at his feet.

Still more people came, waving branches they had pulled from the palm trees alongside the road. They sang:

"Hosannah! The son of David! He comes in the name of the Lord! Blessed is he!"

"Don't let them say such things about you, Master!" said a Pharisee, who was shocked that the people should be so happy. But Jesus answered:

"I tell you that if the people were silent the stones would cry out to welcome me!"

He entered the Temple, followed by a great crowd of people, singing and waving palms. The Temple guards and the scholars and lawyers were outraged.

"Stop that shouting!" they said, but no one took any notice. The priests and lawyers turned away in anger.

"He must be arrested!" they said. "He is leading the people into rebellion!"

Jesus Drives the Money Changers out of the Temple

Jesus went into the Temple. To the right and left of him squatted beggars, stretching out their hands to him. Jesus spoke to them, and gave them his blessing. In the forecourt sat the blind and the lame; they were not allowed to come any further. Jesus healed them and passed on.

He came to another courtyard. Here the smell and the noise resembled a cattle market before the Passover. Rams were straining at their chains; kids and lambs butted and trembled in their pens, while doves and pigeons beat their wings against their cages trying to fly out and escape. Most people did not bring their own animals to sacrifice, so all these creatures were waiting to be bought and killed as offerings to God.

Above the noise of the frightened beasts could be heard the shouting and swearing of the men who owned them. From time to time an animal would break loose and its owner would chase it through the crowd, roughly pushing aside the people who had come there to pray.

He, in turn, would be laughed at by the money changers who sat in long rows at their tables, with piles of coins stacked in front of them.

Jesus stood still. He must have remembered the words of the prophet Malachi: *"Suddenly the Lord will come to the Temple . . . and he will cleanse the Temple . . . ."*

He made a rough whip out of some cord that was lying on the ground. Then he raised his arm and brought the whip down on the piles of coins, so that they rolled across the yard. He scattered the cages, so that they burst open and the birds flew away. He raised his whip in the direction of the traders, and they left their goods and ran out of the Temple. He kicked down the pens, so that lambs and kids scampered into the streets. Finally he overturned the tables themselves, and scattered their benches in disorder.

"Take all this away!" he cried.

The priests and the Temple guards came rushing to see what had happened. When he saw them, Jesus cried in a voice of terrible anger:

"It is written in the Scriptures '*My house shall be a house of prayer for all people.*' But you have made it into a den of thieves!"

The Last Supper

Jesus took Peter and John aside and said to them:

"It is time to prepare the Passover supper. Go into Jerusalem, to the well of Siloam. You will meet a man there, carrying a pitcher of water. Follow him, and when you reach the house he enters, say to the master of the house, 'Our Master says, My time has come. I will celebrate the Feast of the Passover in your house.'"

Peter and John did as Jesus said. They were led to an upper room, with a low table in it, set round with three benches—just enough room for thirteen people. They laid out the food prescribed for the feast: bitter herbs and nuts, raisins and figs, vinegar, salt and a jar of wine. The oil lamps were trimmed, the unleavened bread was baking in the oven. Only the lamb was missing.

When all was ready Jesus came. He brought the other apostles with him, and they climbed up the stone staircase to the upper room. Below them lay the city, its people filled with happiness as they celebrated their release from slavery in Egypt. It was their night of salvation and freedom.

Jesus went to the head of the table. He gave the blessing and passed around the bitter herbs, dipped in vinegar. Suddenly he stood up, took off his long robe and tied a towel around himself like a servant. He took a basin and a jar of water and began to wash the feet of his disciples. Peter exclaimed:

"Lord! You mustn't wash my feet!"

Jesus kneeled in front of him. "Unless you let me wash you," he replied, "You cannot share what is going to happen to me. I am making myself humble before you and you must make yourselves humble before others.

Servants and masters are equal in the eyes of God."

When he had washed their feet and dried them, he took the flat, unleavened bread in his hands. "Praise be to you, Oh God, who have made the bread come from the earth," he said. But instead of adding the usual words the Jews spoke at the blessing, "This is the bread of misery which our fathers ate . . ." he held it up and said, "This is my body, which I am giving for you." Then he broke it, and shared the pieces among them.

He poured the red wine into the big cup, and thanked God with these words, "Praise be to God, who feeds the world with his goodness, grace and mercy." Then he added, "This is my blood, the blood of the New Covenant, which is poured out for men."

They each drank in turn from the cup that he handed them. He was giving his life for the people, he was pouring it out for them so that they could live new lives.

Nothing now would separate them from the love of God. Jesus had given them the New Testament.

Jesus Predicts His Betrayal

JESUS looked at the twelve men he had chosen to share his last supper on earth.

"Indeed, indeed, I tell you, tonight one of you will betray me," he said.

They were filled with horror. "Not *I*, Lord?" each one of them said. John, who was sitting on his right, said, "Lord, which one of us is it? Please tell us."

Jesus replied, "It is the one to whom I will give this piece of bread that I have dipped in the dish." He gave Judas Iscariot the bread and Judas exclaimed, "Surely you don't think *I* would betray you, Lord?" Jesus replied, "It is you who have said it."

The supper drew to its end. "I give you a new commandment," said Jesus. "Love one another as I have loved you. There is no greater love than this—that a man should lay down his life for his friends. You are my friends.

"When I have left you, I will send the Holy Spirit to take care of you. He will help you and guide you in everything that is true.

"Be prepared for people to hate you. But after darkness will come light, after sorrow, joy, and after grief, gladness.

"I am part of you and God is part of me. Now I pray to my Father that he will make us all one together."

Jesus Prays in the Garden of Gethsemane

"COME," said Jesus, "It is time to go." They walked through the sleeping city towards the Mount of Olives. When they reached the valley they heard the sound of water flowing over stones. It was the river Kedron. Jesus crossed the water. He turned to the disciples and said:

"This night you will all desert me. It has been prophesied, '*The shepherd, the companion of God, will be struck down and the sheep of his fold will be scattered.*' That hour has now come."

Peter cried, "Everyone else may desert you, but not I! I will give my life for you; I will suffer anything for you!"

Jesus said sadly, "Indeed, I tell you: this night, before the cock crows twice, you will disown me three times."

Peter cried, "No, never! Even if it means dying with you, I will never disown you!"

"Nor will I! Nor will I, Lord!" they all exclaimed.

They came to the garden of Gethsemane. It was surrounded by a wall, which had a gate in it. Jesus said to his disciples:

"Rest here while I go into the garden to pray."

He took with him into the garden Peter, James and John, who were the closest to him of all his disciples. Then he said to them:

"My soul is deeply troubled, and my heart is breaking. Stay here, and keep watch for me."

He seemed to be in terrible distress and misery as he moved away from them. He threw himself to the ground. With his face against the earth he prayed:

"*Abba*–Father, everything is possible for you. Do not, I beg you, make me drink this cup full of agony and death. Yet, I know it is not my will, but yours, that must be done."

The disciples wanted to go to him in his distress, but he had told them to stay behind. They watched him and waited, but their eyes were heavy with sleep.

When Jesus returned, his disciples were all asleep. He woke them and said to Peter:

"Simon, can you not keep watch for me for one hour? Your spirit is willing, but your body is weak. Watch and pray that you do not fall into temptation."

Again Jesus left them and went deeper into the garden. Again he sank to the ground and bowed low before God. His agony grew in him as he prayed, until the sweat poured from him into the earth like drops of blood.

He returned to his disciples. In their grief and tiredness they had fallen asleep once more.

For the third time he fell to the earth and prayed.

"Your will be done, Lord," he said.

Then he rose and came back to the disciples yet again. "Are you still sleeping?" he said to them. "Look! My betrayers have come!"

The Betrayal

"Come," Judas had said to the Temple police, "And I will take you to Jesus. The man I kiss will be Jesus himself. Seize him!"

They came through the garden gate, carrying torches and lanterns, swords and sticks.

Judas went up to Jesus. "Greetings, Master!" he cried, and kissed him.

Jesus replied, "Judas, my friend, why are you here? Do you betray the Son of Man with a kiss?"

The men drew their swords and closed in on Jesus. Peter barred the way; he struck at the high priest's servant and cut off his ear.

"Put back your sword in its sheath," Jesus said to him. "He who lives by the sword dies by the sword." He turned to the servant and touched his ear, and it was healed. Then he said to the men:

"Who are you looking for?"

"For Jesus of Nazareth," they replied. He said to them, "I am he."

The Temple police came forward. They bound his hands behind him with a rope, pulled off his headcloth and tore at his clothes.

Jesus said to the captain, "I am no criminal. You had no need to come for me in the night, armed with swords. Besides, you can see me every day teaching in the Temple. Why don't you arrest me there? Is it because you are afraid? Yes, this is the right time for you—the hour when everything is dark."

He looked around him. The disciples had run away and deserted him. He was alone with his enemies.

Peter Disowns Jesus

WHEN Jesus was taken prisoner, Peter followed him at a distance. He kept well back from the Temple guards and the soldiers, because he did not want them to see him and arrest him too.

They led Jesus to the palace of Caiaphas. Peter came into the courtyard and drew near to the fire that the guards had lit. He hoped to catch a word or two about what they would do to Jesus.

One of the maids who served in the palace came past. She looked curiously at Peter and then stopped.

"Weren't you one of his men?" she asked suspiciously.

"No, never!" exclaimed Peter.

He got up. The girl shrugged her shoulders and turned away. Peter hid himself in a dark corner of the yard. The voices died down again and there was silence.

In the distance a cock crowed.

Peter began walking towards the palace gate. He was anxious to escape before anyone else recognized him.

He reached the gate. The soldier standing guard there was talking to a servant girl and Peter tried to slip past them both without being seen. But the light of the guard's torch fell on his face, and the girl called out:

"You're one of them! You were with Jesus of Nazareth, and now you're running away!"

"No, no, no!" Peter exclaimed. "I don't even know the man! And I'm not running away!"

"Of course you are," said the guard. "You even speak the same dialect as he does. You're from Galilee!"

"I swear to you I don't know Jesus!" Peter shouted. He pushed past them through the gate and ran down the hill towards the dark city.

Suddenly he stood still. He could hear nothing but the pounding of his own heart.

In the distance a cock crowed again.

Then Peter remembered Jesus saying to him only a few hours before:

"Before the cock crows twice, you will disown me three times."

And he wept bitterly.

The Trial and the Mockery

AT LAST Jesus was in his enemies' hands. He was brought before the Jewish High Court of Justice, the Sanhedrin. Its members took their places in a semicircle and began questioning him. They called one witness after another, trying to find some evidence which would justify them in condemning Jesus to death. There were plenty of witnesses, but their evidence was all false. Finally two men came forward to say that Jesus had blasphemed against God. "He said that he could pull down God's holy Temple and build it up again in three days if he wanted to," one of them insisted.

Caiaphas looked at Jesus. He said in a loud voice, "I charge you to tell us whether you are the Messiah, the Son of the Living God."

Jesus answered, "I am he, and you shall see the Son of Man sitting on the right hand of the Almighty Power."

Then Caiaphas tore his cloak, as if to show that Jesus' words, like the torn cloth, could never be changed. He said:

"What need have we of further evidence? You have heard the blasphemy with your own ears. What is your verdict?"

The members of the Sanhedrin stood up. One after another they said: "He must be put to death." Then they too tore their cloaks from side to side.

Jesus was taken away. The guards beat him with their fists, and hit him in the face.

They spat on him, and then threw a cloth over his head so that he could not see and struck him again.

"Now prophesy," they jeered, "who was it who hit you?"

The Sanhedrin had no power to condemn Jesus to death; only the Roman governor, Pontius Pilate, could do that. So they led him to the governor's palace.

"What is this man accused of?" asked Pilate.

"He leads people astray and forbids us to pay taxes to Caesar. He also claims that he is the Messiah, the king of the Jews."

Pilate looked at Jesus. His clothes were torn and shabby. He certainly didn't look like a king.

"Are you the king of the Jews?" he asked.

"It is you who have said it," replied Jesus.

"This man is no criminal," said Pilate. "Why should I punish him on your flimsy evidence?"

He added, "Anyway, he's from Galilee. That is King Herod's province. Let Herod judge him."

So Jesus was taken to Herod. The king asked him many questions, but Jesus would not answer them. The priests and scholars of the Sanhedrin stood around Herod, trying to persuade him that Jesus was dangerous, that he was a political leader who threatened the power of Rome. Herod looked at Jesus. He was disappointed with him for not letting even one little miracle happen before his eyes. He waved the members of the Sanhedrin away.

"Take him back to Pilate!" he said. "I don't want to condemn him!"

Herod's soldiers began to jeer. They dressed Jesus in fine clothes, like those of a king in the circus, and led him around the courtyard, making fun of him.

The Crucifixion

Jesus was brought before Pilate once more. The Roman governor summoned the chief priests and leaders of the Jews before him and said:

"I cannot see why Jesus should be put to death. If you like, I can have him beaten, and then release him."

But the crowd that had gathered outside was gripped in a kind of fever. The people began to yell:

"Away with him! Free Barabbas instead!" They knew that Barabbas was a thief and a murderer, but they preferred him to Jesus. So Barabbas was freed. But the crowd still wanted Jesus to die. They howled:

"Crucify him! Crucify him!"

Pilate was afraid of this mad and evil mob, and tried to shout them down. When they took no notice of him, he called for a basin of water and washed his hands in front of them, so that they could see, even if they wouldn't hear, what he meant.

"I will have nothing more to do with you all. I wash my hands of your affairs. From now on you yourselves are responsible for what happens to Jesus of Nazareth!"

The Roman soldiers led Jesus away and beat him. When he was half dead they put a red robe on him, plaited a crown of thorns and pressed it down on his head. They put a reed in his right hand as a sceptre. "Look at the king of the Jews!" they laughed.

Pilate led Jesus out so that everyone could see him. He called in Latin, "*Ecce Homo* – behold the man! Here is your king!"

Jesus was taken out of the city. He was made to carry the cross on which he would be crucified. On it someone had written in Greek, Latin and Hebrew:

"Jesus of Nazareth, King of the Jews."

He was by now so weak that he fell several times as he carried the cross. Then the Romans made another man who was standing in the crowd, Simon of Cyrene, carry it for him.

People lined the roadside as the procession climbed up the stony hill to a place that was called Golgotha, which means "place of a skull," because it was the ground where criminals were executed. There a woman came forward, bringing Jesus a cup of wine mixed with myrrh to deaden his pain, but he did not take it.

The soldiers nailed him to the cross with a nail through each hand and through his feet. As they hammered the nails in, he said, "Father, forgive them, for they do not know what they are doing."

Then they set the cross up on end so that Jesus' weight hung from his pierced hands and feet.

The soldiers shared out Jesus' clothes between them, and cast the dice to decide who should take his robe.

John, his disciple, stood close by with a couple of women, supporting Jesus' mother. Jesus said to him, "She is your mother now." To Mary he said, "He is your son."

Two convicted thieves were crucified too, and their crosses set up on either side of Jesus. Despite his pain, one of them jeered at Jesus. But the other said to Jesus, "Remember me when you come to your kingdom." Jesus replied, "Today you will be with me in heaven."

Some members of the Sanhedrin murmured, "If he really is the Messiah, he will save himself. Then we will believe."

Suddenly the wind rose in the east and the sun was darkened. The people fled in terror.

Jesus cried, "My God, my God, why have you deserted me?" He was repeating words from one of the songs King David had written long before, which continue:

"*Let those who seek the Lord, praise him, and be glad in their hearts for ever. I shall live for all time, and shall serve him!*"

The Roman soldiers who had crucified Jesus and the thieves had brought some wine to drink during the long time they would have to wait for the men to die. It was rough and sour, but it quenched the thirst.

Jesus murmured, "I am thirsty."

One of the soldiers soaked a sponge in the wine and stuck it on his spear so that Jesus could wet his dry lips.

Jesus sucked a little wine from the sponge. Then he fell back against the cross.

"It is finished!" he said.

He cried out with a loud voice, "Into your hands, Lord, I commit my spirit."

Then his body died on the cross.

The Resurrection

AFTER Jesus had been crucified, two of his friends, Joseph of Arimathea and Nicodemus, took his body down from the cross, as they wanted to save it from a mass grave. Three women quickly embalmed it as it was nearly the Sabbath, when no Jew could work. Then they carried the body to a tomb cut out of the hillside rock, laid it there wrapped in linen, and rolled a great stone across the entrance.

When the Sabbath was over, Mary Magdalen and two other women set off towards the tomb again to anoint Jesus' body more carefully. It was dark and no one saw them. Then, as the night lifted, a light rose in the east. The women stood still, looking at the tomb. The stone was no longer in front of it. It had been rolled away.

They walked fearfully towards the dark mouth of the cave. They leaned in to see better. A young man was there, dressed in a bright, white robe. He said:

"Do not be afraid. Are you looking for Jesus who was crucified? He is not here." He pointed to the side of the tomb. "That is where they laid him. He is gone from here. Why do you look for the living among the dead? Remember that he told you while he was still in Galilee that he would rise again on the third day."

The women were overcome with terror. They ran back to the house where the rest of the disciples were staying and cried out to Peter:

"They have taken the Lord out of the tomb, and we do not know where he is."

Peter and John ran up to the tomb to see for themselves. John ran ahead, leaving Peter behind. He looked into the tomb. By now the sun had risen and its rays fell deep into the inside of the rock.

John saw the winding sheet lying there, but he was too awed to go in. Simon Peter came up. He ran past John, into the cave. The linen strips that had been wound around the body lay on one side, while the cloth that had covered his head lay on the other. They puzzled about what it could mean, and then they returned to the city.

Mary Magdalen had stayed near the tomb, weeping and mourning for Jesus. Then two angels appeared before her. "Woman, why are you crying?" they said to her.

"They have taken away my Lord and I do not know where he is!"

She looked around and saw a man standing nearby. "Woman, why are you crying?" he said.

Supposing that he must be the gardener, Mary answered:

"Sir, if you have taken him away, tell me, please, where he is, so that I can carry him away."

"Mary!" he said to her.

Mary looked at him. "*Rabboni!*" she cried, "Master!" For it was Jesus.

"You must not touch me now," he said. "I have not yet gone to my Father. Go and tell the others that I am going to my Father and your Father, to my God and your God."

The Disciples See Jesus

THAT same day two of the disciples left Jerusalem for Emmaus. While they were deep in conversation about the recent events, Jesus himself came and walked along the road beside them but they did not recognize him. He said:

"What are you talking about so seriously?"

They said sadly, "Haven't you heard all the things that have happened in Jerusalem?"

"What things?" asked Jesus.

"Oh, about Jesus of Nazareth. How our priests and rulers have had him crucified . . . what's more, some of our women have been to the tomb and have seen angels there, who say he has risen from the dead."

Jesus said, "Do none of you understand that the Messiah must suffer all this so that the prophecies can be fulfilled?"

They reached Emmaus. The disciples said, "Stay with us, please. Darkness is falling. It will soon be night."

He sat down at the table with them, and took a loaf of bread. He gave thanks to God, broke it in pieces and gave the pieces to them. Then their eyes opened wide.

"It's Jesus!" they exclaimed. But before they could say any more Jesus had disappeared.

They hurried to Jerusalem to tell the others: "Jesus is risen! We have seen him!"

Doubting Thomas

THE apostles did not expect to see Jesus again once he was buried. They found it difficult to believe the men and women who said they had seen him.

"You only saw what you wanted to," they said. "You imagined everything!"

The men who had seen him at Emmaus insisted, "He broke bread with us, and we recognized him!"

Suddenly Jesus was there, in their midst. The doors were locked for fear of the Temple police. No man could have come through them.

"Peace be with you!" he said. "Why are you worried, and why do you doubt me? Look at the marks in my hands where the nails pierced them. Feel me; I am no ghost."

Thomas, one of the twelve, was not there that evening. When the others told him later, he would not believe them.

"Unless I see the marks of the nails in his hands and feet, I shan't believe it," he said.

A week later they all met again, and this time Thomas was with them.

Suddenly Jesus was standing in their midst.

"Peace be with you!" he said. Then he looked directly at Thomas. "Put your finger here, in the wounds in my hands and body. Then you will believe."

"My Lord and my God!" cried Thomas.

"You believe because you have seen me," Jesus said to him. "Happy are those who can believe even without seeing me."

The Ascent into Heaven

JESUS remained on earth for 40 days after his resurrection, showing himself to his disciples and to those who had loved him during his life on earth. There were some among them who still did not dare to believe that he had returned. Then, when they saw him with their own eyes, they fell on their knees and worshipped him.

He had done everything that the prophets in the Old Testament said he would. He had brought light into the world, and had won them back to God by dying for them on the cross. He had founded his kingdom. He had brought love and joy and peace into the world.

On the last day Jesus led his disciples to a hill outside Jerusalem. He raised his arms and blessed them. Then he said:

"All power on heaven and on earth has been given to me. You must go now, and call new disciples to follow you from all the nations of the earth, and baptize them in the name of the Father and of the Son and of the Holy Spirit. Teach them to do everything I have told you to do. And remember, I will always be with you, even to the end of the world."

As he said these words, a cloud came down from heaven and hid him from their sight. The cloud became a light, and the light filled the sky and the earth, and covered everything on the earth with glory.

The Beginning of the Church in Jerusalem

JESUS had said, "Stay in Jerusalem until God sends you power from on high."

The city was filled with pilgrims who had come for the feast of Pentecost. It was the day of thanksgiving for the wheat harvest and for the giving of the Law to Moses.

God chose this day to send his Spirit into his people, to found his Church, and give them his new law of love.

The disciples were all gathered together when suddenly there came from the sky a rushing noise like that of a great wind. It filled the house where they were staying. Tongues of fire appeared, which settled above the head of each of them. They were filled with the Holy Spirit, and began to speak in all the languages of the world about God and his love. People gathered in the street outside to ask what was going on.

Peter came out to them and said, "My friends, the prophecy has been fulfilled that says, *'God pours down his spirit on all people; young men shall see visions; old men shall dream dreams.'* So repent, and be baptized in the name of Jesus Christ, and then you can have your sins forgiven and receive the gift of God's Holy Spirit."

More and more people were baptized and joined in the fellowship of the Church. They met every day and broke bread together in their homes, and shared simple joys, constantly praying to God.